ed

Piqua Public Library
116 West High Street
Piqua, Ohio 45356

THE BUDDHAS OF BAMIYAN

WONDERS OF THE WORLD

....

THE BUDDHAS OF BAMIYAN

LLEWELYN MORGAN

Harvard University Press
Cambridge, Massachusetts
2012

First published in the United Kingdom in 2012 by
Profile Books, Ltd.
3A Exmouth House
Pine Street
London EC1R OJH, U.K.

Typeset in Caslon by MacGuru Ltd

Designed by Peter Campbell

Library of Congress Cataloging-in-Publication Data

Morgan, Llewelyn.
The Buddhas of Bamiyan / Llewelyn Morgan.
— 1st Harvard University Press ed.
p.   cm. — (Wonders of the world)
"First published in the United Kingdom in 2012 by Profile Books . . . London"
—T.p. verso.
Includes bibliographical references and index.
ISBN 978-0-674-05788-3 (cloth : alk. paper)
1. Bamiyan Site (Afghanistan)   2. Buddhist antiquities—
Afghanistan—Bamian (Province)   3. Buddhist sculpture—Afghanistan—
Bamian (Province)   4. Gautama Buddha—Statues—Afghanistan—Bamian
(Province)   5. Bamian (Afghanistan : Province)—Antiquities.   6. Bamian
(Afghanistan : Province)—History.   7. Bamian (Afghanistan : Province)—
Description and travel.   8. Religion and culture—Afghanistan.   9. Religion
and politics—Afghanistan. I. Title.
DS375.B36M67   2012
958.1—dc23   2012006342

For Alan MacDonald,
the outstanding staff of MACCA,
and everyone else involved in mine clearance
in Afghanistan and around the world

CONTENTS

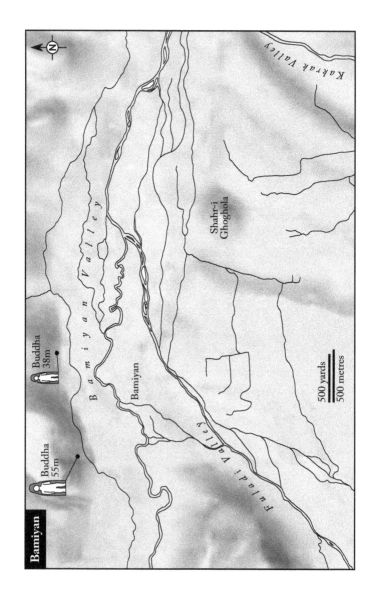

Bamiyan

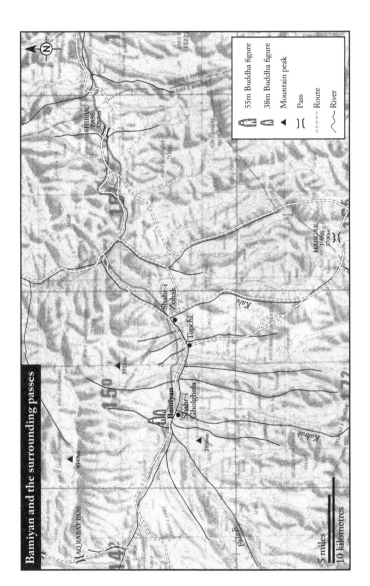

Bamiyan and the surrounding passes

55m Buddha figure	
38m Buddha figure	
Mountain peak	▲
Pass	)(
Route	=====
River	~~~

SHIBAR PASS 2987m

SHAHR-I ZOHAK

Topchi

HAJIGAK PASS 3700m

Kalu

391m

Bamiyan

Shahr-i Gholghola

2386m

Kabdak

4349m

MAQ RABAT PASS

Falak

5 miles

10 kilometres

←N

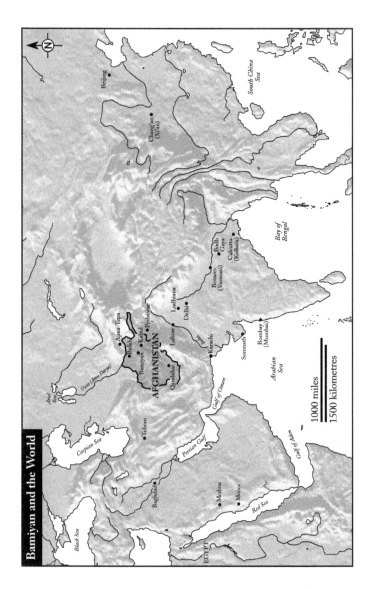

Bamiyan and the World

FOREWORD

This is a book about a monument, an astonishing monument, a wonder of the world. But this wonder no longer exists.

The Buddhas of Bamiyan were carved out of a cliff face in Afghanistan 1,400 years ago, and these vast creations, towering over their remote mountain valley, had amazed and mystified countless visitors ever since. Then, in early 2001, the Buddhas were demolished on the instructions of Mullah Muhammad Omar, leader of the Taliban, a movement which combined Islamic fundamentalism with Pashtun nationalism (the Pashtuns being the largest of Afghanistan's many ethnic groups). By 2001 the Taliban had seized control of most of Afghanistan, and had outraged the West by granting sanctuary to Osama bin Laden. Before the end of 2001 the Al-Qa'ida attacks on 9/11, plotted on Afghan soil, would lead to the toppling of the Taliban regime.

In the following chapters we will discover why these statues were carved in the first place. We will visit the flourishing Buddhist kingdom of Bamiyan, which in the sixth and seventh centuries exploited the commercial advantages of its location, and a period of stability (in this perennially unstable region), to enlarge an established Buddhist community and construct two colossal and elaborately decorated images of the Buddha. By the tenth century Islam had supplanted

Buddhism at Bamiyan: we will explore what these statues had meant to the Buddhists who saw and worshipped them in their heyday as objects of religious devotion (from the sixth to ninth centuries), but also the intense interest they continued to provoke in the Islamic world that followed, deeply intrigued as it was by the Indian cultures it encountered on its eastern border. When the dramatic upheavals of the twelfth and thirteenth centuries (culminating in Genghis Khan's annihilation of Bamiyan in 1221) brought a new population to the valley, the Buddhas once again found a place in the folk tales of the Hazara people (another of Afghanistan's ethnic groups), in whose ancestral homeland, the Hazarajat, Bamiyan is located.

Visitors of an entirely different kind arrived in Bamiyan in the nineteenth century, adventurers and spies heading to or from British India, bringing with them a whole new set of cultural assumptions but sharing the same fascination for the Buddhas. The history of Bamiyan is never simple – often, in fact, dizzyingly complex – but the unfailing power of this monument to excite the passionate interest of witnesses – to be regarded as a Wonder, and as such demanding a remarkable explanation of its existence – in the seventh, eleventh or twentieth centuries, by Buddhists, Muslims or Christians, is a common thread we can follow through it. Indeed, the Buddhas of Bamiyan can sometimes seem the only thing left untouched by this valley's tumultuous past.

They were not allowed to remain untouched for ever, of course. The Bamiyan valley is still today a magnificent place, one of the most beautiful and remarkable sights on the planet. But the Buddhas, properly speaking, are no longer part of it, and the story of these enigmatic statues must begin at the end, with the catastrophic events of February and March 2001.

1

....

DYNAMITE AND CELEBRITY

*But that day will not bring back the things we loved: the high,
clear days and the blue icecaps on the mountains ... We shall not
lie on our backs at the Red Castle and watch the vultures wheel-
ing over the valley where they killed the grandson of Genghiz ...
We will not stand on the Buddha's head at Bamiyan, upright in
his niche like a whale in a dry dock.*

Bruce Chatwin

The footage is poor quality – grainy and a peculiar colour. In
the distance, a cliff and an indistinct carved figure in a niche
surrounded by caves. Then a sudden orange flash, the boom of
an explosion, and, as the shockwave jerks the camera, a thick,
billowing cloud of dust. There are cries of 'Allahu Akbar!',
'God is Great!' from men out of picture.

It is March 2001, in Bamiyan, Afghanistan, and we are wit-
nessing the destruction of the smaller of two colossal Buddhas.
Other footage shows the larger Buddha, already demolished
from the waist down, as its torso explodes. The images were
captured by a journalist from Arabic-language broadcaster Al-
Jazeera, Taisir Alluni, who was subsequently, controversially,
jailed in Spain for collaboration with Al-Qa'ida. In Christian
Frei's documentary *The Giant Buddhas* (2005), Alluni comes

1. The smaller, 38m Buddha at Bamiyan, flanked by caves used by Buddhist monks for prayer and meditation. A staircase in the left-hand wall of the niche gave access to the caves, and led up to a gallery behind the Buddha's head: the staircase and gallery still exist, even after the destruction of the Buddha. This is the first photograph of a Bamiyan Buddha, from J. A. Gray, *At the Court of the Amir* (1895), an account of his time as court surgeon to Abdur Rahman, Amir of Afghanistan at the end of the nineteenth century.

across less as a collaborator than a journalist determined at any cost to secure the story. He confesses to some guilt at his participation, but also admits that the scenes were irresistible to a journalist who 'wanted to get sensational pictures, the big scoop'. Frei presses Alluni for a deeper analysis of the events at Bamiyan. The destruction came after the intensification of UN sanctions against Afghanistan, Alluni answers: the Taliban thought the world had completely abandoned them. They were spitting in the face of a world that did not give a damn about their country, that was more interested in stone sculptures than the thousands of Afghan children who were facing starvation in the winter of 2000/2001. The West had made no attempt to understand the Islamic world in its full, rich complexity, and this was the payback.

These and similar attempts to rationalise the deliberate destruction of the Buddhas of Bamiyan were repeated by commentators across the world in 2001, and have been since – but never very convincingly. In truth, Alluni and Frei and everybody else seemed to be fishing for a satisfactory explanation of an inexplicable turn of events. Even Taliban spokesmen at the time were struggling to account for their leaders' actions, which, apart from anything else, represented a dramatic shift in policy: in 1997 the Taliban ambassador to Pakistan was insisting that 'the Supreme Council has refused the destruction of the sculptures because there is no worship of them'. As late as September 2000, Mullah Omar had issued a clear decree to similar effect: 'The government considers the Bamiyan statues as an example of a potential major source of income for Afghanistan from international visitors. The Taliban states that Bamiyan shall not be destroyed but be protected.' The Taliban leader's subsequent volte-face was bizarre and shocking: to a senior

Taliban commander, Ghulam Muhammad Hutak, 'Mullah Omar's actions seemed pure madness.'

The motivation behind the destruction may have been obscure, but its target was not. Bamiyan was Afghanistan's Stonehenge, the most celebrated archaeological site in the country: two colossal standing images of the Lord Buddha carved from a cliff of reddish conglomerate stone on the north side of a valley high in the Hindu Kush mountains. In their first two centuries of existence, until about 800, the Buddhas were the brightly coloured, flamboyantly decorated centrepieces of a flourishing Buddhist community, as we shall see in the next chapter. By the end of the twentieth century they had endured more than a millennium of natural degradation and human neglect, but they were still exceptionally impressive monuments.

The western, larger Buddha was 55m tall, and its partner 800m to the east, 38m. The larger Buddha, by general consent, was the more photogenic of the two, comparatively better proportioned and less top-heavy: its elegant trefoil niche was also an advance on the rougher niche of the smaller figure. Radiocarbon dating of organic fragments from the statues has recently corroborated suspicions that the larger, more sophisticated figure was also later, constructed around 615, half a century or so after the smaller (c.550). The statues were carved in deep relief, attached to the back wall of their niches from the level of the hem of their clothing up to the backs of their heads, an arrangement which had facilitated the important Buddhist ritual of circumambulation: worshippers could walk around the statues both at ground level, behind their huge bare feet, and behind the tops of their heads. Modern visitors could step out onto their heads. The route around the smaller Buddha's head was well-defined into modern times and still exists today, despite the destruction of the statue, a nerve-wracking stairway within the fragile western side of the niche leading to head-level, then a more gradual path down through the cliff on the eastern side. There was also a gallery around the larger Buddha's head, but no equivalent access in the niche wall (which, as we shall see, foxed some early Western visitors). But it is clear enough that this Buddha too originally allowed visitors to reach its crown, by a path high on the cliff that had been lost to erosion: in the twentieth century a new path was constructed.

The soft, crumbly rock of the cliff is not suitable for fine carving, and thus only the core of the statues had been carved from the rock itself. Embellishments such as hair, clothing and hands had originally been represented by means of a painted clay coating, or appendages moulded around wooden beams anchored in the stone, but most of this more fragile material had disappeared by the twentieth century. How the statues might originally have looked we shall investigate later, but traces of their decoration were still visible in 2001. For example there were remnants of the two layers of clay that had been applied to the rough stone cores: a thick, coarse undercoat and a thin, finer finish coat with a very smooth surface to which paint could be applied. Hundreds of small holes on each Buddha pointed to techniques for helping this coating to adhere to the rock. In the case of the smaller Buddha conical holes peppered the statue, visible wherever the clay had fallen off (on his chin the effect was rather like stubble): these had originally been stopped with stones which anchored the clay facing. On the larger Buddha an intricate technology had been employed which both fixed the clay and represented the folds of the Buddha's *samghati* or outer cloak. On the smaller Buddha these folds had been carved in the rock, but on the later statue pointed pegs 30–40cm apart were inserted into holes and connected by ropes, over which the ridges of the folds were moulded in clay (see ill. 26). Only between the larger Buddha's legs were the folds worked in stone.

The garments of the Buddha were those of a Buddhist monk (of whom the Buddha was the archetype and model), the traditional monastic three-part combination (*tricivara*) of the *uttarasanga*, upper garment, *antarvasaka*, lower garment, and outer cloak, *samghati*, which covered both shoulders and fell down to the figures' shins. So meticulous was the presentation of the clothing on the Buddhas that the inner lining of the *samghati* and folds of the undergarment could be seen where the Buddha's raised arms lifted up the *samghati*. On the smaller Buddha the *antarvasaka* extended down below the lower hem of the *samghati*. The fabric was represented as fine in texture, formed into regular folds, and clinging so tightly to the Buddha's body that his anatomy was visible beneath it. In some places traces of the original bold colour schemes of the statues had also survived.

The forearms of both Buddhas (all but the larger Buddha's left forearm) had originally projected out from the wall, reinforced by beams: in all cases the hands were long gone by the twentieth century, along with their wooden reinforcement, but parts of the lower arms, and the fall of the Buddha's *samghati* from them, did survive. Large sections of the legs of the western Buddha were also missing, and the damage to his left shin and thigh was clearly later than the creation of the statue, though the date and cause were unclear. The large parallel holes on his right shin were generally interpreted as evidence of a later repair of damage occurring soon after the statue was first carved.

The most distinctive feature of the Buddhas of Bamiyan was their faces, blank in both cases from the top of the hair to above the lips, a clean vertical slice. For some viewers the absent faces were essential to the impression they made: 'No statue which has had its face removed can express justice or law or illumination or mercy,' Peter Levi wrote in 1970, 'but there is a disturbing presence about these two giants that does express something.' In actual fact it is a matter of debate whether the faces were removed by medieval Islamic iconoclasts or if this was an original feature of the statues, the prevailing view now being the latter: a trough between the horizontal and vertical planes of the recess on each Buddha's face has been interpreted as an anchoring point for wooden structures – face masks, effectively – that represented their features. The larger Buddha's head was still topped by the Buddha's characteristic cranial protuberance, the *usnisa*, a representation of his transcendent intelligence, and both Buddhas still had parts at least of their pendulous ears (elongated earlobes were a characteristic appendage of the once princely and bejewelled Buddha), moulded in clay, and traces of hair, realistically moulded in wavy curls that betrayed a slight lingering influence from the Greek-influenced so-called 'Gandharan' sculpture which had flourished at the north-western edge of India in the early centuries AD. Even before 2001, it should be said, that description of the Buddhas' heads would require modification. At the end of 1998 zealous Taliban, who had captured Bamiyan shortly beforehand, blew off the head and part of the shoulders of the smaller Buddha. At around the same time tyres were burned on the ledge above the larger Buddha's mouth, blackening its 'face'. At this stage the Taliban leadership had been a restraining influence, and the destruction was not allowed to go any further.

In between the two colossal Buddhas were three smaller niches for seated Buddha statues. All remains of images within them were destroyed by the Taliban, but until 2001 one of the three had still contained isolated fragments of its original statue, while another had preserved the whole core of its image, which had evidently been constructed by a technique similar to that used for the larger images: the surface of the figure was studded with holes which presumably anchored the more perishable material from which the visible image was moulded. The cliffs all around the Buddha niches are honeycombed with caves, over 700 in total, also dating back to the Buddhist period when they served as chapels and places of prayer and meditation. In more recent times many of them had served as homes for local people – until the cliffs became an officially designated archaeological site in the twentieth century – and as a result the roofs and walls of a lot of the caves were blackened with smoke. But still in the twentieth century a number of caves and both Buddha niches retained extensive traces of the complex religious painting which had originally covered much of the walls and ceilings. In the soffit of the smaller niche, for example, were paintings of a mysterious figure in a horse-drawn chariot and a series of individually characterised royal donors, represented seated on a balcony adorned with embroidered rugs and making offerings to the Buddha: presumably a representation

2. The most complete of the seated Buddhas at Bamiyan, as rendered
by the celebrated journalist and war artist William Simpson for the
Illustrated London News, 13 November 1886, on the basis of a sketch by
Capt. P. J. Maitland, an officer with the Afghan Boundary Commission.
Maitland and another officer, M. G. Talbot, surveyed the arduous 'central
route' through the Hindu Kush from Herat to Kabul, but of Bamiyan an
enthusiastic Maitland insisted that 'to see these antiquities alone was worth
all the trouble of the journey'.

of the Buddhist dynasty responsible for the carving of the statues. The boldness of conception of the Buddhas, and the obvious commitment of resources their construction entailed, inevitably makes the identity of these men a matter of great interest. But it is not a question we can answer in any detail, since, whoever they were, they left no record of themselves beyond these tantalising images. What we can say is that the construction of the Buddhas and other developments in the Buddhist complex at Bamiyan seem to coincide with the hegemony of a regional power known as the 'Western Turks', a multi-ethnic confederation of essentially nomadic tribes which brought a degree of stability (and economic prosperity) to central Asia, including Bamiyan, from the sixth century on. We will explore this shadowy but important historical territory in the next chapter. Many of the paintings in the caves were vandalised during the Taliban occupation of Bamiyan. All of the paintings in the niches, needless to say, were destroyed in the explosions that demolished the statues.

GIANTS AND PYGMIES

A detailed description like that is all well and good, and only to be expected at the beginning of a book about a monument of this kind, but what it cannot convey is the raw impact that these statues had on visitors for nearly one and a half millennia, the smallest hint of which still comes today from gazing up into the towering, empty niches. The Buddhas of Bamiyan were truly colossal, and the sheer overwhelming scale of these sculptures without fail drew superlatives from viewers even if they did not particularly warm to what they saw. The challenge has always been to convey their size, and the impulse of every visitor has been to attach a measurement to them, whether in Chinese *chi*, Persian *gaz* or English foot, while even their most articulate detractors, Goethe and Robert Byron, talked of 'crazy idols … on a gigantic scale' and their 'monstrous flaccid bulk'. What none of us now have the opportunity to do is actually experience the Buddhas of Bamiyan in person, but that makes us much like the British readers of the 6 and 13 November 1886 issues of the *Illustrated London News*, in which the famous war artist William Simpson had the task of introducing new information about this distant and inaccessible monument collected by British officers of the Afghan Boundary Commission. The Boundary Commission was a group of military surveyors engaged, theoretically at least, in drawing up a stable boundary between the British and Russian spheres of influence: as we shall see, a disproportionate number of British visitors to Bamiyan in the nineteenth century were military surveyors. The theodolites and measuring tapes of these officers in 1886 had now for the first time produced accurate measurements of the statues, respectively 173ft and 120ft (53m and 36.5m), although even these precisely calculated figures had to be adjusted to 55m and 38m in the 1970s when the Archaeological Survey of India led excavations which, among other things, fully exposed the Buddhas' feet.

To give flesh to these numbers Simpson adopted an inspired journalistic strategy. He imagined that 'a general meeting of all the colossal statues of the world' could be called, bringing together the Colossi of Memnon from Luxor in Egypt ('they are 51ft high, and would be taller if they could stand up out of their seats'); the four statues of Rameses II from Abu Simbel ('about 50ft high'); the bronze Japanese Buddhas at Kotuku-in (13m; 44ft) and Todai-ji (15m; 49ft); 'the statue

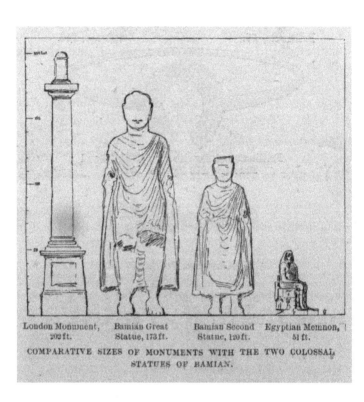

London Monument, 202 ft.   Bamian Great Statue, 173 ft.   Bamian Second Statue, 120 ft.   Egyptian Memnon, 51 ft.

COMPARATIVE SIZES OF MONUMENTS WITH THE TWO COLOSSAL STATUES OF BAMIAN.

3. Illustration from William Simpson's description of the Buddhas of Bamiyan in the *Illustrated London News*, 6 November, 1886. The larger and smaller Buddhas are set against the London Monument (which commemorates the Great Fire of 1666), one of the 'Colossi of Memnon' from Luxor in Egypt – and a tiny human figure at the far right.

of Athene made by Phidias for the Parthenon, which was 39ft in height; or the Olympian Jupiter, by the same artist, 6oft high, a statue celebrated for its great size, as well as for its perfect workmanship'; and 'the still greater Colossus of Rhodes, the records of its height varying from 100ft to 120ft'. But if the larger Buddha at Bamiyan were to stroll into this AGM of ancient colossi, 'what pigmies most of them would then seem!' 'The colossal Apollo of Rhodes, one of the Seven Wonders of the World, would lose all pretence to superiority in height as he had to look up 53ft – at the lowest estimate – to the gigantic strangers from Bamian.' Simpson concludes with a contemporary touch: 'The new "Liberty" statue at New York is 105ft high, on a pedestal of 83ft, but [with] the raised hand and torch, 137ft.' Appropriately for the *ILN*, only London is allowed to claim a monument taller than the larger Buddha: an image accompanying Simpson's article sets the two Buddhas, sketched with an unprecedented accuracy by one of the surveyors, Captain P. J. Maitland, against a Colossus of Memnon on one side and the 202ft (61m) London Monument (commemorating the Great Fire of 1666) on the other – with a minuscule human figure to scale.

Simpson's parade of Wonders, we can agree, is a brilliantly creative variation on pure measurement, and gets us closer to grasping the massiveness of these statues. But if there was a competition to convey the sheer impact of the Buddhas, the prize would surely go to Edmund Melzl and his photograph, taken in 1958, of a VW Beetle parked tidily between the feet of the larger Buddha. Melzl, a sculptor by profession, has had a long involvement with Afghanistan, and since 2003 has been engaged in preserving and cataloguing the fragments of the Buddhas left after their demolition. But he first went

4. Edmund Melzl's photograph of a German construction worker's VW Beetle parked between the larger Western Buddha's feet in August 1958.

to Bamiyan with his parents when his father was employed in the construction of a cotton textile plant near Kabul, the capital of Afghanistan: this was a period when strenuous efforts were being made to give the country a modern industrial infrastructure. During their holidays the German workers would head up into the mountains, to Bamiyan and the nearby beauty spot at Band-i Amir, and it is one such whose car was snapped by Melzl.

'ALL FAKE IDOLS MUST BE DESTROYED'

Forty years later, in altogether darker circumstances, it was the size of the Buddhas of Bamiyan that ensured they were destroyed. On 26 February 2001 Mullah Omar issued the damning edict:

On the basis of consultations between the religious leaders of the Islamic Emirate of Afghanistan, religious judgments of the ulama [senior clergy] and rulings of the Supreme Court of the Islamic Emirate of Afghanistan, all statues and non-Islamic shrines located in different parts of the Islamic Emirate of Afghanistan must be destroyed. These statues have been and remain shrines of unbelievers and these unbelievers continue to worship and respect them. God Almighty is the only real shrine and all fake idols must be destroyed. Therefore, the supreme leader of the Islamic Emirate of Afghanistan has ordered all the representatives of the Ministry of Promotion of Virtue and Suppression of Vice and the Ministries of Information to destroy all the statues. As ordered by the ulama and the Supreme Court of the Islamic Emirate of Afghanistan all the statues must be destroyed so that no one can worship or respect them in the future.

Even before Omar's decree, Taliban had entered the National Museum in Kabul on 12 February and smashed statues; they would return on 17 March, after which they invited international news media to inspect their handiwork. A 15m reclining Buddha discovered by Italian archaeologists at Ghazni was also smashed, but once the Taliban had embarked upon this campaign of destruction, the fate of the Bamiyan Buddhas, by far the most prominent 'idols' in the country, was sealed.

In the event, it was a massive operation to demolish the Buddhas, and it took weeks. Twenty foreign journalists were finally flown to Bamiyan to see the empty niches on 26 March, a full month after Mullah Omar's decree. The details of the process are obscure, for it was witnessed by no Western journalists, but what is clear is that it needed a series of detonations to destroy each of the sculptures. Dynamite, artillery, and anti-aircraft weapons were turned against the statues. We are told that the demolition team ran out of explosives and had to request that more be brought in, and that they were relieved when they found an ammunition store abandoned by the military opponents they had driven out of Bamiyan. One report claims that they were only finally successful when expert Pakistani and Arab engineers were brought in, at which point a professional job was done of drilling holes in the statues and inserting explosives. It is certainly true that local inhabitants, despised on ethnic and religious grounds by the intensely sectarian Taliban (an aggressively Pashtun and Sunni movement, while the people of Bamiyan are predominantly Shi'a, and from the Hazara ethnic group), were forced to drop down by rope and lay charges in the statues. When archaeologists came to sift the rubble after the fall of the Taliban, there was so much unexploded ordnance still lying around that they had to be preceded by mine clearers. Countless other acts of vandalism took place around the huge Bamiyan complex. For example the core of the seated Buddha which had survived a hundred metres west of the 38m Buddha was blown up, along with some particularly vividly coloured paintings on the ceiling of its niche. But if we can force ourselves to contemplate dispassionately vandalism on such a scale, the most peculiar aspect of it is the massive commitment of resources, in an impoverished country embroiled in an ongoing civil war, to the demolition of what the Taliban foreign minister (Omar's confidant and one-time official spokesman) dismissed in a press conference on 18 March as 'some statues of stone'. Some very big statues of stone, big and solid enough to survive the vagaries of history that will fill the rest of this book, well over a millennium of regular earthquakes and brutal winter weather especially. To the French archaeologist Albert Foucher, in 1922, they had seemed as indestructible as the very flanks of the mountain that hosted them. Big and solid enough to make it very hard to bring them down, which only sharpens the question: why?

CUI BONO?

We have already heard some of the favoured explanations from Taisir Alluni, the Al-Jazeera journalist. The Taliban were lashing out after the tightening of sanctions (which were designed to force them to surrender Osama bin Laden), or were reacting to the (alleged) lack of Western concern for the millions of Afghans under threat of starvation. Others have suggested that the Taliban were taking revenge on the

Hazara people of Bamiyan, their military opponents and religious and ethnic rivals, or else that they were simply following through the logic of their own narrow religious ideology. Each of these explanations was regularly aired, but none of them ever quite stacked up.

One problem is that Mullah Omar's movement didn't care enough about the outside world to be interested in 'spitting in its face', as Alluni put it. James Fergusson has drawn an essential distinction between the Taliban and Al-Qaʻida: 'Mullah Omar's movement was filled with Afghan Pashtuns with an exclusively domestic agenda; bin Laden's was manned by Arabs whose goals were international.' Nor was the welfare of the Afghan people, as many as five million of whom were under threat of starvation in early 2001, any kind of priority for the Taliban. Had it been, they might have heeded the particularly impassioned pleas on behalf of the Buddhas by Japan, a country which was a major humanitarian donor to Afghanistan; or they might have accepted the money offered by Western institutions to preserve Afghanistan's antiquities. To the latter approach Mullah Omar's response on the Voice of Shariʻa (as Radio Kabul had been renamed) was, 'Do you prefer to be a breaker of idols or a seller of idols?' – an echo of an archetypal iconoclast, the eleventh-century Mahmud of Ghazni, who was said to have refused a huge ransom for a Hindu image in similar terms. In reality, what typically drove the Taliban's actions was a messianic determination to impose their primitive idea of Islamic practice, and this motivation seemed to override any other consideration. The Pakistani journalist Ahmed Rashid, an expert on modern Afghanistan, describes Taliban measures in 2001:

The Taliban also escalated tensions with the UN and aid agencies, passing new laws that made it virtually impossible for such agencies to continue providing relief to the Afghan population. The Taliban shut down Western-run hospitals, refused to cooperate with a UN-led polio immunisation campaign for children, and imposed even more restrictions on female aid workers, such as preventing them from driving cars. The Taliban arrested eight Westerners and sixteen Afghans belonging to a German aid agency and accused them of trying to promote Christianity, a charge punishable by death.

How far could this religious zeal take them? Far enough to punish the Hazara people of Bamiyan, who were Shi'a and thus heretics in the eyes of the Taliban? The Taliban did extract increasingly brutal revenge for the resistance put up by the Hazara organisation, Hizb-i Wahdat, whenever they captured or recaptured Bamiyan and adjacent areas. So was the destruction of the Buddhas also part of these campaigns? Again, it doesn't seem likely. The Buddhas did not occupy such a central role in Hazara culture that their destruction could count as an attack on Hazaras. But if, on the other hand, the actions were a straightforward expression of the Taliban's extreme notion of piety, as many Taliban insisted, what had made them change their minds about this, when the arguments they had made earlier to preserve the Buddhas remained perfectly valid?

They were certainly left in no doubt that theirs was a minority view among Muslims: Islamic nations were among those that begged them not to proceed with the demolition, and a deputation of eleven senior Islamic clergymen even visited Qandahar in an attempt to persuade Mullah

Omar that the proposed action had no basis in Islamic law. Their message was rejected, and the clergymen, some of the foremost authorities in the Islamic world, were personally insulted. One of the leaders of the delegation, Yusuf al-Qaradawi, commented that the Taliban 'had absolutely no knowledge about Islam. They are so naïve, they really can be influenced.' It could not have been more clearly stated to the Taliban, and to the world in general, that the destruction of the Buddhas was not an Islamic act.

Perhaps the Taliban's religious zeal is sufficient to explain the events at Bamiyan in 2001, but two things suggest otherwise: the unmotivated change of policy from their earlier unambiguous statements that the Buddhas were under no threat, and the intensely provocative nature of the course of action that was adopted. It was quite obvious that destroying the Buddhas would provoke outrage outside Afghanistan, and as James Fergusson saw, the Taliban's agenda was essentially domestic: they had no interest in provoking the attention and outrage of the world, and indeed seemed a bit nonplussed at the storm of protest that did follow the destruction. Al-Qaradawi's suspicion, shared by many others, was that the process was driven by figures other than the naïve Supreme Leader of the Taliban, and that suspicion has hardened in the years since. Jason Burke, in his authoritative book *Al-Qaeda*, writes that 'Mullah Omar's decision to destroy the huge statues of the Buddhas at Bamiyan … appears to have been taken after a concerted lobbying campaign by foreign militants inside Afghanistan supported by a series of fatwas from Wahhabi clerics in Saudi Arabia'. Ahmed Rashid is more specific: it was 'at the encouragement of bin Laden' that Mullah Omar ordered the destruction. What is revealed by a close analysis of developments within the Taliban leadership in the run-up to 9/11, such as the scrupulously researched *How We Missed the Story* by journalist Roy Gutman, is the growing influence over Mullah Omar exerted by Al-Qaʻida and its leader Osama bin Laden, notwithstanding the quite fundamental differences between the two organisations. At the same time as bin Laden issued ever more aggressive challenges to the US, he was also making himself indispensable, financially, militarily and even psychologically to the Taliban leadership: more than one account of these events have talked of the 'hijacking' of the Taliban regime. Arab fighters, logistics and military know-how played a major role in the significant Taliban advances into northern Afghanistan in the second half of 1998, including the capture of Bamiyan, and in 1999 informed analysts were talking of an effective merger of Al-Qaʻida and the Taliban: in the words of a US ambassador to Pakistan, 'Omar became a bin Laden convert, a believer in bin Ladenism.' 'Increasingly,' describes Ahmed Rashid, 'bin Laden's world view appeared to dominate the thinking of senior Taliban leaders. All-night conversations between bin Laden and the Taliban leaders paid off.' The influence of 'the Arabs' (as the Al-Qaʻida fighters were known in Afghanistan) was particularly intense in the run-up to the demolition of the Buddhas, reports talking of Taliban making ostentatious visits to the National Museum in Kabul to slap Buddhist images as the Al-Qaʻida agenda took over. Nilab Rahimi, director of the Kabul public library, has described a group of Taliban removing hundreds of books deemed inappropriate, assisted by an unidentified Arab (that is, an Al-Qaʻida operative) with a computer. Mullah Omar quoted Mahmud of Ghazni again in a telephone conversation with Mullah

Rabbani, the titular head of the Taliban government, who was trying to dissuade him from destroying the Buddhas: 'I am not the sculpture seller. I am the sculpture destroyer.' Friends were advising him, Omar told Rabbani: Arabs and two mullahs from Karachi. One of the mullahs was certainly Rashid Ahmad, the founder of the extremist Al-Rashid Trust and publisher of an Urdu-language Islamist newspaper which later produced a celebratory calendar with photographs of the demolition process. Among the Arabs, equally certainly, was bin Laden.

Al-Qa'ida, as one expert on Afghanistan has put it, 'has always practised the propaganda of the deed'. 'Al Qaeda, which has never had roots in social movements, ceases to exist if it isn't on the front pages and on our television screens.' Finbarr Barry Flood has pointed out both how an act of iconoclasm like this is characteristic of the hardline Wahhabi branch of Islam espoused by bin Laden, and also how, for all the Taliban rhetoric of a return to pristine Islamic values, the destruction of the Buddhas, followed by the flight of those twenty foreign journalists to the site, 'was a performance designed for the age of the Internet'. 'Performance' is the right word. Al-Qa'ida atrocities have always had a theatrical quality about them, what the journalist Lawrence Wright has characterised as a perverse kind of artistry, designed 'not only to achieve the spectacular effect but also to enlist the imagination of the men whose lives bin Laden required'. Wright cites the terrorist's own reading of the suicide attack on the USS *Cole* in Aden harbour in October 2000, in which a small fishing skiff loaded with explosives nearly sank an 8,300-ton, billion-dollar American warship: 'Two men brought the tiny skiff to a halt amidships, smiled and waved, then stood at attention.' The symbolism and the asymmetry of this moment were exactly what bin Laden had dreamed of. 'The destroyer represented the capital of the West,' he said, 'and the small boat represented Mohammed.'

One of the sources of bin Laden's appeal to certain constituencies was his skill in working within a well-established Islamic symbolic language, the modelling of actions on religious or historical paradigms. Adam Silverstein comments on another of his statements: 'when Osama bin Laden compared the US-led invasion of Iraq to the Mongol conquest of the region in the 1250s, he was striking an historical chord that has rung continuously over the past 750 years. The Mongol destruction of the Abbasid caliphate has endured in the *umma*'s [the global Muslim community's] collective memory just as the Battle of Hastings survives among the British.' More recently, Olivier Roy has described the 'media circus' that followed bin Laden's death as 'merely the act of a great actor who died on stage playing his final role', a man whose primary achievement was to secure the unwavering attention of the Western media. The 'performances' aimed to elicit contrasting reactions in its audiences, of course: support from one constituency, and outrage and (over-)reaction from the other. Fundamentally, bin Laden wanted to provoke 'a clash of civilisations' – many might say that he achieved some success. What is most telling about the attack on the USS *Cole* is that bin Laden was positively disappointed when the United States *failed* to react militarily.

The destruction of the Buddhas of Bamiyan, on the other hand, was an immensely successful act of provocation, generating a global storm of protest, the dominant news story across the world. It was also a powerful recruiting tool: the number of foreign Al-Qa'ida volunteers arriving in Afghanistan increased tenfold in the following month. It was performative in other respects, too. The scholar of religion Jamal Elias has pointed out how carefully the events of March 2001 were timed to correspond with the Hajj, the pilgrimage to Mecca, and the associated festival of Eid al-Adha, both of which carry special associations with Abraham, the original opponent of idolatry, who asked his father Azer, a maker of idols, in the words of the Qur'an, 'O my father, why do you worship that which does not hear and does not see and will not benefit you at all?' In retrospect, a disturbing further connection occurred to some. In the 15 July 2002 issue of the *New Yorker*, the artist and illustrator J. Otto Seibold responded to an invitation to imagine a fitting memorial on the site of the Twin Towers: his image depicted the two Buddhas of Bamiyan recreated in Manhattan, while miniature Twin Towers, housing refugees, occupied the empty niches in Bamiyan. It may be hard at first to see any point of similarity between New York City and the placid, green, undeveloped space of the Bamiyan valley, or indeed between 100-storey constructions of steel, concrete and glass and the clay-coated stone of the Buddhas, but radical Islamism might see things differently. A buzzword of Islamist radicals since Said Qutb, the influential thinker executed by Egyptian authorities in 1966, is *jahiliyya*, denoting the 'state of ignorance' which preceded the mission of the Prophet Muhammad, and motivated his work, but which also by extension continues to exist in the ungodliness and immorality of the West, or in excessively secular regimes in the Islamic world. To this mindset, that starkly delineated space outside the very narrow confines of 'true' Islam could equally well be symbolised by the Twin Towers, embodiments

5. J. Otto Seibold's proposal for refilling the site of the Twin Towers, from the *New Yorker*, 15 July, 2002: the two Buddhas are rebuilt in New York City, while Twin Towers, accommodating refugees, occupy the empty niches at Bamiyan. From a radical Islamist perspective, the two acts of destruction might indeed seem related, both being attacks on cultures perceived to be opposed to the 'true' Islam they claim to espouse.

of the hegemony of Western values ('Those awesome symbolic towers that speak of liberty, human rights, and human-
ity,' as bin Laden put it in an interview), or the two Buddhas
of Bamiyan, arguably the most impressive representations in
the world of the idolatry that Islam had superseded.

CELEBRITY

Whatever motivated the destruction of the Buddhas of
Bamiyan, it had the effect, outside a comparatively small
group of sympathisers, of outraging sentiment in the wider
world. In predominantly Buddhist countries such as Japan
or Sri Lanka, there were special local reasons for that. In
the wider developed world the reaction was also guaranteed
by its commitment to the preservation of 'heritage', which
has evolved into the principle, somewhat muddily conceived, of a common human cultural heritage, enshrined in
UNESCO's Hague Convention of 1954: 'damage to cultural
property belonging to any people whatsoever means damage
to the cultural heritage of mankind'. (Bamiyan was belatedly
inscribed on the UNESCO World Heritage List in 2003,
and simultaneously added to the List of World Heritage in
Danger.) At the time of the destruction claims to the effect
that the Taliban were destroying not just Afghan heritage
but something that belonged to everyone on the planet were
treated as uncontroversial. At least some of the perpetra-
tors of the destruction will have anticipated the storm that
did in the event break worldwide, ironically because of the
strong representations which had been made by foreigners,
such as the representatives of the Society for the Protection
of Afghanistan's Cultural Heritage (SPACH), calling for the

protection of the Buddhas and other pre-Islamic material in the country. SPACH had helped to shape the Taliban leadership's earlier, conciliatory view of the Buddhas, and had even prevailed upon Hizb-i Wahdat, the Taliban's opponents in the fight for Bamiyan, to relocate an ammunition dump located at the base of the larger Buddha. With hindsight, a decision by SPACH to reopen the National Museum in Kabul for six days in August 2000, a clear advertisement of the importance attached by Westerners to Afghan antiquities, may not have been the wisest move.

But if the brief exhibition in 2000 gave some people an idea, the deeper insight here is that in 2001 it was surprisingly easy for people in the West to be persuaded that the Buddhas of Bamiyan were a matter of concern to them. On 8 March *The Economist* could with every reason complain how depressing it was 'to observe that the world seems to care more about the destruction of two stone statues, which – let's be honest – hardly anyone had even heard of until ten days ago, than about 100,000 refugees who have been starving and freezing to death near Herat a few hundred miles away from them'. One thing we shall trace in the remaining chapters of this book is the periodic spasms of celebrity enjoyed by the Buddhas of Bamiyan, in the Buddhist and early Islamic periods, and again in the mid-nineteenth century, and we will note a tendency for renewed interest in these monuments to coincide with renewed attention to the strategic value of the location they occupied (hence all those British surveyors passing through, for example). But we will also see that with the Buddhas' fame in the Muslim or Christian world came a seemingly irresistible impulse to possess. The deep paradox of the destruction of the Buddhas in 2001 is that the dynamite and ordnance also inaugurated Bamiyan's fourth and greatest era of celebrity, and their apotheosis as the treasured monuments, not merely of Bamiyanis or Afghans, nor even of Buddhists, but of the entire global community.

2

....

REIMAGINING BAMIYAN

If they employ pigments to paint Buddha images,
Endowing them with the characteristics of hundredfold merit,
If they make them themselves or have others make them,
Then all have attained the Buddha way.

From the Lotus Sutra

In 1968 the artist and Hiroshima survivor Ikuo Hirayama visited Bamiyan. 'I went there,' he explains, 'to seek the origins of Japanese culture and to follow the way that Buddhism diffused. I also wanted to share the same experience as the Chinese Buddhist monk, Xuanzang, who travelled in and around India for eleven years to deepen his insight into Buddhism.' Getting to Bamiyan from Japan in the 1960s, Hirayama soon discovered, was far from straightforward. But eventually his ambition was realised:

When I … visited Bamiyan from Kabul by car one evening, I got a very powerful and unforgettable impression from the caves of Bamiyan. I sat on a bank in front of the Great Cliff, looking at the caves between the 55 m high West Giant Buddha and the 38 m high East Giant Buddha, and immersed myself in drawing rough sketches of them until sunset. The next day I explored mural

[29]

paintings in the caves around the East and West Giant Buddhas remembering ... what Xuan Zang wrote ... He mentioned that in those days, Buddhism was so prosperous in Bamiyan that there was a statue of [a] golden Giant Buddha there and the dwellings of numerous monks. I remember I was thinking about such things as I made sketches of the site, broadening my imagination while in awe of its breathtaking beauty.

Over the fourteen centuries of their existence the Buddhas of Bamiyan were an object of fascination for people of many faiths. In this book we will hear the responses to Bamiyan of the Islamic cultures that succeeded to Buddhism in north-west India and central Asia, and then of the Christians who visited when the British were extending their control of the Indian subcontinent. But our point of departure must be the Buddhist origins of Bamiyan, and a representative of a contemporary Buddhist culture such as Ikuo Hirayama is an excellent first voice to hear. In this chapter we shall also be relying quite heavily, as Hirayama did, on the information left us by Xuanzang, a Buddhist monk who travelled from China to India, via Bamiyan, in the seventh century and whose exploits made him as famous a figure in the East as Marco Polo is in the West.

What Hirayama has in common with every visitor to Bamiyan, of every faith, is what led him, that day in 1968, to sketch the cliffs until the light gave out. Enter the valley of Bamiyan and you are met with a quite astonishing view, best captured by the travel-writer Robert Byron in the 1930s as 'the colours of this extraordinary valley with its cliffs of rhubarb red, its indigo peaks roofed in glittering snow and its new-sprung corn of harsh electric green'; 'there suddenly, like an enormous wasps' nest, hung the myriad caves of the Buddhist monks, clustered around the two giant Buddhas'. An arresting sight to this Western visitor, at an earlier point in history the power of the view of the cliffs holding the Buddhas contributed to an intense religious experience. Hints of this come in Xuanzang's account of his visit, which we shall come to later in this chapter, but the most authentically religious response to the sight of the Buddhas is preserved (interestingly) in Arabic by a Muslim, in a tenth-century literary compendium, the *Fihrist* of Al-Nadim:

The people of India [i.e. non-Muslims] go on pilgrimages to these two [idols], bearing with them offerings, incense and fragrant woods. If the eye should fall upon them from a distance, a man would be obliged to lower his eyes, overawed by them. If he is lacking in attention or careless when he sees them, it is necessary for him to return to a place from which he cannot view them and then to approach them, seeking them as an object for his attention with reverence for them.

To most non-Buddhist visitors too, like Lieutenant Vincent Eyre, a prisoner of the Afghans trudging exhausted into Bamiyan in September 1842, the view that met their eyes was awe-inspiring:

Seven miles more took us to Bameean, the approach to which was very remarkable. The same clay hills lined the valley on either side, alternating in shade from deep red to bluish grey, and forming here and there long lines of perpendicular cliff.

The vast assemblage of caves, for which the place is celebrated, became visible at a great distance, and the ancient city

6. An Afghan banknote with a panorama of Bamiyan, 1939. This was the first series of Afghan notes to carry different images for each denomination, and Bamiyan's presence on the two-Afghani note (the first in the series) is a sign of Bamiyan's growing role in assertions of Afghan nationhood, which owed a lot to the work of French archaeologists in the valley.

of Gulguleh, with its lofty ruined towers, crowning an isolated pyramidal hill, rising behind the scene, formed a striking and imposing object … The whole long line of excavations forms a wonderful scene, and carries the fancy back thousands of years, to a date at which a widely different race peopled the country from any now existing.

Eyre, a talented amateur artist, made a number of sketches of Bamiyan, which were later published alongside the bestselling account he wrote about his ordeal. But the stunning views have flattered much more pedestrian efforts than Hirayama's or Eyre's to convey them, and since practically every visitor has felt a compulsion to record the view, there are quite a few of those. Another example of an accomplished image of the Bamiyan valley graced the very first Afghan issue of banknotes to carry images, in 1939: a sign of Afghanistan's pre-Islamic history, and Bamiyan in particular, being drawn for the first time into expressions of an Afghan national identity. But if to all visitors the scene is arresting, and to some beautiful, to others the Buddhas and the caves around them were disorienting and disturbing. The Buddha images and the art decorating the niches and caves could be alien and incomprehensible, especially to the Western eye: of the idols 'I have little to say', writes the no-nonsense author of an article on 'The Mountain Passes leading to the Valley of Bamian' in 1879 (recalling a military expedition forty years earlier), 'except that they are very large and very ugly'. Robert Byron, in 1934, managed to react both ways, waxing lyrical on his first day in Bamiyan, as we have seen, but remarking on the following day (perhaps he had eaten something that disagreed with him), 'I should not like to stay long at Bamian … Neither

(Buddha) has any artistic value ... their negation of sense, the lack of any pride in their monstrous flaccid bulk, ... sickens.' Dr James Gerard, who accompanied the most glamorous nineteenth-century visitor to Bamiyan, the explorer and spy Alexander 'Bokhara' Burnes, certainly was ill (he did not long survive the expedition), and that no doubt partly explains the feverish quality of the vision he describes:

> *the sides of the mountains are full of excavations, presenting to the approaching traveller some thing like a honey comb; whole families occupy these recesses, living in smoke and darkness, of which they seem to form a part, in their black figures. – One of the idols is actually tenanted, and high upon the acclivity are seen isolated nitches and black heads peeping forth. At night, the moving lights and yells of unseen people have a singularly wild effect, and one dwells in the contemplation of the scene, till it actually appears one of an infernal kind, fit only for such companions as bhuts and demons.*

'Burnes took sketches of the whole,' Gerard adds, and Burnes's account of Bamiyan was also considerably sunnier, though that was partly because Burnes was consciously writing for a public, while Gerard was confiding his feelings to private letters. Gerard's reaction, nightmarish as it is, is still an authentic response to the extraordinary quality of this monument, its power to compel by its very strangeness.

THE VIEW FROM THE HILL

But let us take up our own position, and get our bearings in this place which so demands to be *seen*, and about which,

7. A view of the Bamiyan valley from the hill known as Shahr-i Gholghola, 'City of Hubbub' (see ill. 16). The larger niche is visible on the left, and the smaller on the right, both at least two kilometres distant. The town of Bamiyan can be seen in the valley, and the dense vegetation to the right of the picture marks the course of the Bamiyan river.

out of all places, it may plausibly be said that its geography is its destiny. We are standing at the top of the odd conical hill to the south-east of the Buddhas, the site of the Islamic-era citadel known as Shahr-i Gholghola, 'City of Hubbub', according to tradition a reminiscence of its violent capture by Genghis Khan. We have taken the winding path to the summit, and done so with confidence now that the NGO tasked with clearing the mines and unexploded ordnance that used to litter the site, the ATC demining agency, has completed that tricky work: what was a strongpoint a thousand years ago was a defensive position again in the recent civil war. From this elevated position we have a commanding view northwards over the Bamiyan valley. Dominating the scene are the ochre cliffs of sandstone and conglomerate, north-west of us, dotted with caves and punctuated by the two huge niches of the giant Buddhas, that of the 55m statue to the west, and of the 38m statue 800m to its east. They are both easily visible with the naked eye even though the closer one is a couple of kilometres away from us. This is partly a consequence of their size, and partly of our altitude. Above the cliffs rise the high peaks of the Hindu Kush, perpetually under snow, and at Bamiyan we are already very high up: the valley lies at about 2,500m above sea level. The light has a high-altitude intensity, and the sun in May is unforgiving.

Between our position on Gholghola and the Buddha cliffs, the valley of the Bamiyan river is green and well cultivated, the river itself (and its tributary the Fuladi) marked by a fringe of poplar trees. The landscape is predominantly agricultural, oxen ploughing the fields, but the narrow strip of the main street of Bamiyan town, the bazaar, cuts across the valley in front of us, a large school at its eastern end: the figures most noticeable at this distance are schoolgirls in white headscarves. We may pick out some other archaeological remains, fragments of fortifications around us on Gholghola, and dotted along the valley, and just to the east of the eastern niche a peculiar masonry formation, known to locals as Tolumbai, which has been well described as looking like a 'stone mushroom', but which in fact marks the remains of one of the most celebrated buildings of medieval Bamiyan, the Great Stupa. We can see the remains of another stupa (a reliquary mound with a tower-like vertical extension central to Buddhist worship and ritual) just below Shahr-i Gholghola itself.

A slightly broader perspective will be helpful, too. Behind us, against the backdrop of the Kuh-i Baba mountains, the valley of Kakrak branches off to the south, the site of more caves and another large Buddha (six to seven metres tall, his feet on lotus leaves), also destroyed in 2001. Here, radiocarbon dating suggests, the practice of Buddhism may have persisted after it had given way to Islam in the main valley, perhaps even into the tenth century. To the west of our position, a low plateau above the valley base holds the air strip, and behind that the base of the New Zealand contingent of the ISAF forces (the NATO-led international military presence in Afghanistan), who have responsibility for Bamiyan province. Beyond the plateau, heading south-west, is another tributary valley, Fuladi (heard as 'Fool'ardy' by the British captives in 1842, a name that seemed to mock their plans to escape). Here also caves point to a once thriving monastic community, and one that may again, by virtue of its seclusion, have survived longer than in the main valley.

If we could borrow one of the ISAF helicopters which occasionally clatter overhead, we could get a broader perspective still. From above we would see the network of roads, from north, south and east, which converge on the valley. Visitors to Bamiyan, especially visitors at the end of a bone-jarring road trip along the unmetalled roads from Kabul (Bamiyan thrived in the era of the camel, not the motor car), or visitors whose arrival coincides with winter, when the fertility of the valley is less in evidence, struggle to understand 'the enigma presented to us by the unexpected existence of these monuments in a territory that is mountainous and poor, and of which the least one could say is that it lies fifty leagues from anywhere' – the words of Alfred Foucher, founder of the French archaeological mission in Afghanistan, who visited in November 1922. An oblique but fascinating insight into the sheer expense of carving and embellishing the Buddhas has come from recent research into the wood extensively used in their construction, in all likelihood a rare and precious commodity in the environment of sixth- and seventh-century Bamiyan. Which makes all the more urgent, and at first sight unfathomable, the central 'problem' of Bamiyan: where did the small kingdom which ruled this valley in the Buddhist period find the resources for such an ambitious building project? Why are these remarkable monuments 'lost in the midst of a vast ocean of mountains' (Foucher again)? Part of an explanation is that Bamiyan has a hidden source of wealth today, and apparently also had it in the past, in the shape of major mineral deposits under these very mountains. A huge source of iron ore is set to be exploited at Hajigak, south-east of Bamiyan, for example, and in the fourteenth century the geographer Mustawfi tells us of a district in Bamiyan 'called the Iron Foundry'; tantalising recent archaeological discoveries have pointed to metalworking alongside other industrial activities in the Buddhist period. But the real key to Bamiyan's existence is the geographical position of this fertile and pleasant valley, at a nexus of routes across the massive mountain barrier of the Hindu Kush. Some fifteen kilometres to our east, perched dramatically on red cliffs, stands the fortress of Shahr-i Zohak, described by one scholar as 'that Afghan Krak of the Chevaliers', which governs access to the Bamiyan valley. Beneath Shahr-i Zohak alternative roads from Kabul meet, from the south and east (via the Unai and Hajigak passes, and the Shibar Pass), and other routes from the south meet the Bamiyan valley between Shahr-i Zohak and Bamiyan itself. Meanwhile, at the western end of the valley, a road north, over the Aq Rabat Pass (and a series of further passes including Dandan-Shikan, a difficult crossing whose name translates as 'The tooth-breaker'), leads towards the plains north of the Hindu Kush, and the cities of Balkh and Mazar-i Sharif. Whoever held Bamiyan thus effectively controlled movement along these critical arteries of trade, conquest and religious proselytism over the Hindu Kush.

There is also a wider network to consider. In Bamiyan we are roughly halfway between Balkh and Peshawar, which means halfway between the Indian subcontinent and central Asia, from where important routes led on to the West or to the East and China. We may, if we like, employ an overused term and describe the route through Bamiyan as a branch of the Silk Road. But at any rate the fundamental reason for Bamiyan's prosperity is that memorably formulated by Thomas Holdich, a military surveyor with a particular expertise in Afghanistan (to which he helped to give the long north-eastern extension known as the Wakhan Corridor, essentially a mechanism to keep the British and Russian Empires apart):

*That a confined narrow ribbon of space such as Bamian, difficult
of access, placed by nature in the heart of a wilderness, should
have been the centre not only of a great kingdom but the focus of
a great religion, would be inexplicable if we did not remember
that through it runs the connecting link between the wealth of
India and the great cities of the Oxus plains and Central Asia.*

This pivotal physical position boasted by Bamiyan was
enough to provoke even the sceptical Robert Byron to exclaim
that 'Geography has its excitements'. What set Byron's pulse
racing was driving from Bamiyan towards the Shibar Pass,
on the eastern route to Kabul. The Shibar is the watershed
between two great river systems drained by the Oxus (Amu
Darya) and the Indus, so that as Byron reached the Shibar
Pass, 'we left the last trickle of the Kunduz, as it started on its
long journey to the Oxus and the Sea of Aral. Five minutes
later another trickle started on a journey to the Indus and
the Indian Ocean.' Babur, the first Moghul emperor, but at
an earlier stage of his remarkable career based in Kabul, captures the pivotal geographical position of Bamiyan even more
vividly:

*The Bamian mountains and [a mountain near Kabul] form part
of a single chain, and the Helmand, the Sind, the Dughaba of
Konduz, and the Balkhab rivers all have their sources in this
range. In a single day it is possible to drink from the waters of
all four rivers.*

Babur's 'Dughaba of Konduz' is the continuation of the
Bamiyan river, a tributary of the Oxus, as originally was the
Balkh, which is now diverted into irrigation schemes before

it can reach the larger river. By the 'Sind' or Indus, Babur meant the Ghurband (Byron's second 'trickle'), which joins the Kabul river, which in turn meets the Indus, while the Helmand heads south towards the province of the same name. What all this means is that Bamiyan sits at the heart of a formidable physical barrier between India and Inner Asia and provides comparatively easy passage through it. If we describe this in the most abstract terms possible – as the meeting of the Iranian plateau, north and west of Bamiyan and the Indian subcontinent to the east and south – we can see how it might end up that in the Buddhist period at Bamiyan (most of the first millennium AD), an essentially Iranian people were following an essentially Indian religion, guarding the boundary of traditionally Iranian and Indian cultural spheres.

BETWEEN BALKH AND KABUL

Predictably enough, this strategic position has made Bamiyan a perennial bone of contention for powers on either side of the Hindu Kush. Bamiyan's control of a major trade route ensured that it received two types of visitors in particular: the *qafela* or *karavan* (one an Arabic, and one a Persian word for a merchant's convoy) – and armies. An American visitor in 1838 can illustrate both: the adventurer Josiah Harlan, who passed through the valley twice on a punitive expedition, undertaken at the behest of the Amir of Afghanistan, against slave traders based north of the Hindu Kush. Heading north, Harlan and his army provided protection to 'a great karrovan of 1,600 camels and 600 pack horses, together with 2,000 souls' carrying 'Cashmere shawls, indigo, white and printed piece goods' to Mazar-i Sharif, the day-to-day supplies for the convoy having been 'provided chiefly at the station of Bameean'. But heading in the other direction a few months later, what had been a welcome source of security had become something much more malign:

> *As the population became more numerous on our approach to Bameean, forage was procured with increased difficulty. The natives had not sufficient for the subsistence of their cattle until spring. They buried their grain and hid their hay in ravines and we were obliged to force these necessaries from them by revolting cruelties in a few instances. The cry was 'Thou shalt want ere I want' and the maxim was carried out with robber-like ferocity.*

Both scenes and circumstances, the lucrative convoy and the pillaging soldiery, have been regular features of Bamiyan's history, and whatever else its position ensured, violent incursions have been the fate of the valley from time immemorial until the present day. Geographically, and for most of its history also politically, Bamiyan has had its strongest links to the north, to Balkh especially. This great central Asian city, called the 'Mother of Cities' in deference to its supposedly immense age, became a major centre of Buddhism and will be mentioned repeatedly in this book, a constant point of reference in the history of Bamiyan. A sign of its importance is that the paths of the three great travellers of the medieval world, Islamic, European and Chinese – Ibn Battuta, Marco Polo and the Buddhist monk Xuanzang – all crossed at Balkh. Much earlier another iconic wanderer, Alexander the Great, had captured Balkh in 329 BC, and later he married the famous Roxane, the daughter of a local commander. But in recent centuries Bamiyan has tended to fall within the ambit of Kabul, to the south-east of the mountains, now the capital of Afghanistan. The deeper geographical truth of Bamiyan, however, is that its position in the middle of the highlands has made any attempt to exert control over it, from either north or south, tenuous. The characteristic condition of Bamiyan is a nominal fealty to greater powers, but an effective (though vulnerable) autonomy. That fundamental, geologically imposed isolation, and concomitant independence, is reflected in the survival of Buddhism here long after adjacent territories had converted to Islam. Later, as the anthropologist Thomas Barfield suggests, 'it is no accident that the core Shia and Ismaili populations in Sunni-dominated Afghanistan are found in its most remote mountain regions': the Hazaras of Bamiyan are Shi'a, and have suffered great historical injustices as a consequence. But equally, as Barfield goes on, the highlands are themselves inherently disunited places: 'When Bamiyan was Buddhist, monks in the valley undoubtedly complained about the unholy heresies being expounded in the highlands around them.'

BAMIYAN'S MOMENT

So much for Bamiyan's location, but what still requires an explanation is why *this* route across the Hindu Kush (in preference to a number of others) achieved such importance, and after that why it was a *Buddhist* culture that benefited from Bamiyan's rise to prominence. We need to consider some historical developments first, and then turn our attention to less familiar characteristics of the Buddhist religion, in particular its commercial interests. But first a health warning.

The author of the *Beishi*, the Chinese *History of the*

Northern Dynasties, writing in the seventh century, speaks for historians of pretty much any period of Afghan history when he writes despairingly of the period from the mid-third to mid-sixth centuries, 'From the time of the Northern Wei and the Jin, the dynasties of the Western Territories swallowed each other up and it is not possible to obtain a clear idea of events that took place there at that time.' What made the Afghan scene so convoluted in the first millennium (and still does today) was precisely its pivotal geographical position, which ensured that it was the constant object of interest from competing powers, and was constantly changing hands. Fortunately for us, the Chinese chronicler is referring to an especially opaque passage of events which fell just before the time of major activity at Bamiyan. In the period relevant to us, roughly from the second half of the sixth century onwards, things are slightly clearer, and we think we can discern (still rather dimly) the turn of events that gave Bamiyan the prominence it achieved, and the resources and self-confidence necessary to construct the colossal Buddhas.

Most importantly, something happened in the sixth century to redirect commercial traffic between Chinese central Asia and India, which had hitherto crossed the mountains in what is now the very north of Pakistan, westwards towards Bamiyan. In other words, although Bamiyan was the route of choice through the mountains for seventh-century travellers like Xuanzang (of whom we shall hear more later), that had not been the case for very long. The road through Bamiyan will always have had some local significance, and archaeology proves that it had been a Buddhist centre, on a more modest scale, for some time before the Buddhas were carved. But for a traveller from China, especially, the route via Bamiyan represented a significant detour to the west, and it seemingly required some seismic historical developments to turn the Bamiyan road into the major international highway it became in the sixth century. What brought about this change is not absolutely clear (literally seismic events further to the east may have played a part), but what seems beyond dispute is that the growth of Bamiyan as a commercial centre coincides with the expansion of the religious complex at Bamiyan which saw, among other things, the sculpting of the Buddhas: prosperity and Buddhism went hand-in-hand. Fortuitously or not, these momentous developments parallel the rise of a particular regional power, the so-called Western Turks, who exerted for a short period a settling influence on territories either side of the Hindu Kush. It may well have been the influence of this Turkish power that sparked Bamiyan into life, encouraging trade to pass through Turkish territory, which meant through the mountain routes that centred on Bamiyan. If so, Bamiyan was more or less suddenly the beneficiary of peace and a massive growth in trade, circumstances which (the theory goes) prompted the carving of the great Buddhas and the wider development of the Buddhist complex. Such a relatively stable political environment never equates in Afghanistan to an entirely simple one, mind you. Even in this period of comparative peace, Bamiyan was part of a complicated federation of principalities owing allegiance to multiple strata of overlords.

The intricacy of the political structure to which Bamiyan, in its heyday, belonged can be illustrated by a remarkable document that survives in Chinese records. This is a letter of complaint, addressed to the Chinese emperor, written in 718 by Puluo, a Turk of royal blood who was resident at the

Chinese court. He was not being treated with the proper respect, Puluo protested. His older brother was the ruler of a territory roughly corresponding to modern Afghanistan, and that made him the overlord, Puluo reminds the emperor, of numerous kings, governors and prefects, the most powerful of which, Zabulistan and Kapisa, could command 200,000 soldiers and horsemen each. Bamiyan is mentioned among a second level of dependencies, capable of fielding 50,000 men. Given that Puluo's brother was such a powerful and respected figure, and Puluo himself a *tegin*, a man whose 'dignity is considered equal to that of a royal person', it was unacceptable that his position on the strictly regimented Chinese scale of official status was only in the fourth rank. The sons of the kings of Tashkent and Kucha, much smaller kingdoms than his brother's, had been awarded the title of general, in the third rank. 'I cannot overcome the intensity of suffering that I feel at this injustice,' Puluo concludes.

A note follows Puluo's letter in the record to the effect that the emperor ordered Puluo's rank to be set in accordance with the statutes, 'so that he would have no further grounds for complaining of an injustice'. But what Puluo is describing, albeit no doubt in a way that presented his brother in the best possible light, is a version of essentially the same configuration of powers that had been relevant to Bamiyan since the middle of the sixth century. The dominant regional power were the Turks, but such control as they exerted over their vassal kings was superficial. When Xuanzang, the Chinese monk, passed through Bamiyan in about 629, staying a few days as guest of the king, he did so armed with letters of introduction from the Great Khan of the Western Turks, who could clearly command some level of influence over the jumble of principalities in what is now northern Afghanistan. But when the Korean monk Hyecho visited Bamiyan within a decade of Puluo's complaint, no external control was evident to him: 'Its king is an Iranian. He is not dependent on other kingdoms; his foot soldiers and horsemen are strong and numerous: the other kingdoms do not dare to come to attack him.' Thomas Barfield uses the wonderful image of Swiss cheese and American cheese to convey the attitudes to imperial control in play here. He likens modern notions of comprehensive control of an empire to American cheese, with a regular consistency throughout, while pre-modern notions, which allowed for varying degrees of imperial assertion, are like Swiss cheese, full of holes. In the mountains of Afghanistan the pragmatic approach to control of a naturally disunited collection of territories was the Swiss-cheese model, with direct control exerted only in centres. It's easy to see how, to the visitor of a territory in one of these 'holes', like Hyecho in Bamiyan, it might seem entirely independent; but easy also to see how Puluo, when it suited him, could claim to be the close relative of a man to whom it all owed unquestioning obedience.

At the time of Puluo, at least, an entirely different geopolitical layer also needs to be taken into account, as the Turks had their own nominal overlords in the shape of Tang-dynasty China, a token of which was Puluo's own fourteen-year presence at the Chinese court. No doubt China's control of the Turks was as lightly enforced as the Turks' over Bamiyan, but the growth and ebbing of Chinese interest and influence over Afghanistan is another element of a full explanation of the stability that Bamiyan enjoyed in its heyday. There is evidence of diplomatic contact between Bamiyan and the Chinese court even before Xuanzang's visit in c.629, and the art of the Hindu Kush passes through a period of noticeable Chinese influence, most strikingly at the monastery of Fondukistan in the Ghurband valley 130 kilometres east of Bamiyan (seventh to eighth centuries), where the sculptures of a princely couple – the man in central-Asian garb, the woman in Indian – are portrayed in a strange, elongated style betraying Tang Chinese influence. Chinese encroachment would ultimately founder in the face of Arab expansion from the West, but that is a story for the next chapter.

BUDDHISM: A COMMERCIAL ENTERPRISE

The final piece in the puzzle of Bamiyan's existence lies in the nature of Buddhism itself. The critical consideration here is that Buddhist monks were, perhaps contrary to reputation, extremely good at making money. There is a charmingly credulous account by Xuanzang of the relics he saw at Hadda, an enormous Buddhist site (some fifteen square kilometres) near Jalalabad which was the source of some of the most exciting archaeological discoveries in Afghanistan during the twentieth century. If we are to believe Xuanzang, the monks of Hadda were only interested in prayer and meditation, but discovered that in their relics they had what economists call a 'Veblen good', a commodity that is more attractive the more expensive it becomes:

> *The attendants, wishing to spend their time in quietness, and thinking that people would value money more than anything else, made a rule to stop the hubbub caused by the visitors, to the effect that one gold coin should be charged to see the [Buddha's]*

skull bone, and five gold coins for making an impression [in plaster: a kind of fortune-telling]. This rule was also applicable in different grades to the other relics. Although the charges were high, the number of worshippers increased.

In making money out of relics, of course, seventh-century Buddhist monks have some competition in medieval Christian clerics selling indulgences. But the connection of Buddhism with trade goes much deeper than that, and it is no coincidence that Bamiyan, which had been on a trade route of moderate significance since time immemorial, and was then a major commercial centre from the sixth century onwards, was also a flourishing centre of Buddhist worship. Buddhism had a close and longstanding relationship with the merchant class, one enshrined in a founding myth of Buddhism, the story of Tapussa and Bhallika, two merchants who met the Lord Buddha shortly after his enlightenment under the Bodhi tree, and became his first disciples. The brothers reputedly founded the remarkable Shwedagon Pagoda in Burma, and Bhallika also supposedly gave his name to Balkh, the great city north of the Hindu Kush which was a major centre of Buddhism in central Asia. One of the things that the myth of Tapussa and Bhallika explained to Buddhists was the way that their religion had diffused along the trade routes out of India. For whatever reason, as early as Ashoka, the great third-century BC Buddhist ruler of India, a strong relationship was established between Buddhist missionaries and travelling merchants, and that relationship saw monks and missionaries travelling with caravans, and Buddhist monastic foundations unerringly tracking the trade routes, and servicing them. Monasteries offered much more than spiritual comfort: they were hostels, hospitals, bazaars and, most importantly of all, banks, sources of credit and investment which became very wealthy indeed in the process.

Buddhist foundations were intimately involved in the local economy too, investing in agriculture and even industry. A remarkable ongoing archaeological dig at Mes Ainak, south-east of Kabul, is revealing a complex of Buddhist shrines ringing a copper-rich mountain. Currently emergency excavations are taking place ahead of the full-scale exploitation of the copper mine by a state-owned Chinese mining company, the latest stage in the very long history of this economic prize. Mes Ainak was the target of mujahedin attacks during the Soviet occupation of Afghanistan in the 1980s, which destroyed expensive Soviet drilling rigs; more recently some consideration of its commercial potential no doubt occurred to another businessman, Osama bin Laden, who set up a training camp at Mes Ainak in the nineties, graduates of which were among the hijackers on 11 September 2001. Copper mining had also gone on at Mes Ainak in antiquity, and it is clear that the Buddhist site was intimately involved with the copper workings, and that the Buddhist monasteries grew rich from their patronage of the mines. As we shall see in the next chapter, Buddhism's deep roots in the mercantile class also proved to be its undoing when another religion with equally strong commercial instincts, Islam, appeared on the scene. Further afield, it is when commerce withers, as at the great Buddhist cave-site of Dunhuang in western China, which was blighted by the development of sea-borne commerce especially, that monastic centres disappear. Even when Buddhism was flourishing on the trade routes – at Balkh, Bamiyan and Hadda on the way to India – it was always much less in evidence away from the main road. In short, Bamiyan's location makes sound commercial sense (from the mid-sixth century on, in particular); and what makes commercial sense also provided the optimally congenial habitat for a Buddhist community.

RECONSTRUCTING BAMIYAN

We are still atop Shahr-i Gholghola, and by now possibly feeling a bit giddy. But before we climb back down to the car park, past the stones once painted red on one side (danger) and white on the other (safety), but now whitewashed all over, let us try another feat of imagination. For if Bamiyan is a place of stunning views, the view today always demands that we attempt a mental reconstruction. The focus of the complex, the giant Buddhas, are no longer there to be seen. What remains of the larger Buddha now is just a ghostly silhouette on the back wall of the niche and his two huge feet, while the hole where the smaller Buddha used to stand is filled with scaffolding (provided by the Messerschmitt Foundation) associated with work to stabilise the niche. Behind the scaffolding there is a similar ghostly shape of the statue, although this statue retains quite a lot of its right arm and the fall of the *samghati* beneath it. But the important point to appreciate is that in this respect our experience of Bamiyan in 2012 differs only in degree, not kind, from the experience of visitors for at least a thousand years. Bamiyan has always required an effort of imagination, or at any rate has done since it stopped being Buddhist in about the ninth century. To get the full view of Bamiyan we must certainly reimagine the Buddhas as they were before 2001, but we must also go beyond that, recreating from the fragments that remain in Bamiyan as full a picture as possible of the flourishing Buddhist community of its early days.

It is our good fortune that, at the very height of its prosperity as a Buddhist community, Bamiyan received as a visitor the unusually observant Xuanzang, who provides us with a short but vivid contemporary description. In 629 this Chinese Buddhist monk was on his way from Chang'an (Xi'an), the capital of Tang China, to India, frustrated with doctrinal controversies in China and determined to find clarity, the true *Dharma*, in the Buddha's homeland. The journey he undertook was arduous, at times extremely perilous, and it contravened the express orders of his emperor. In the end it made Xuanzang a folk-hero, partly for the enormous contribution he made to the transmission of Buddhist texts to China: setting off alone into the outer darkness beyond the Jade Gate, the edge of the Chinese world, he returned sixteen years later with 657 books bound in bundles requiring twenty packhorses to carry them. But Xuanzang's fame has even more to do with the fictionalised account of his travels in the classic sixteenth-century Chinese novel *Journey to the West*, also known as *Monkey*. A more documentary account of Xuanzang's travels is provided by two contemporary sources: a life of the monk by Huili, based on Xuanzang's reminiscences, and containing the more personal material, and an account dictated by Xuanzang immediately on his return at the behest of the Chinese emperor Taizong (the same emperor who had forbidden the enterprise in the first place). In a fashion rather similar to Charles Masson, the greatest of the nineteenth-century European explorers of Afghanistan, whose talents were used and misused by the British authorities, the scholarly innocent

8. Nineteenth-century silk hanging scroll from Japan, by Ohara Donshu. It illustrates the classic Chinese novel *Journey to the West*, a fictionalised version of Xuanzang's journey from China to India (via Bamiyan) and back in search of Buddhist scriptures. The novel became well known to Western audiences through the cult Japanese TV series *Monkey* in the late 1970s. Here Xuanzang is depicted with his three travelling-companions: a water-imp, a monkey and a pig.

Xuanzang had been drawn into the strategic concerns of the powerful: Xuanzang's highly informative *Da Tang Xiyu Ji*, or *Great Tang Records of the Western Regions*, not coincidentally anticipated Tang China's imperial expansion into central Asia.

So, with Xuanzang as our guide, what do we see? For a start, the predominantly green and agricultural valley before our modern eyes is now covered by buildings. Seventh-century Bamiyan was much more urban than in the twenty-first-century. Up beyond the larger Buddha is the city of Bamiyan, covering most of the valley floor and extending up to the cliff face on the north: a prominent palace within it houses the king, who, according to Huili, entertained Xuanzang for two days on his arrival after a difficult wintry crossing of the mountains from Balkh. Then, from the edge of the city right down to the base of Shahr-i Gholghola, and also behind us in the valley of Kakrak and over in the Fuladi valley, the valley floor is carpeted with monasteries, unmistakable with their cloistered courtyards and stupa towers of all sizes. Xuanzang talks of 'several tens' of monasteries housing 'several thousand monks', but they were built of mud-brick and thus now leave little trace above ground. Even with all the building in the valley, however, the most striking feature, in Xuanzang's day at least, is the cliff face. It looks very different in the seventh century: the comparatively soft rock is highly susceptible to the elements, and the facade has retreated by as much as a metre since that time. Some caves now open to the valley will not have been visible, and there were certainly routes of access which are now lost to us. We might, for example, imagine precarious stone and wooden staircases and walkways running along the face of the cliff, linking the hundreds of caves which are now inaccessible. No doubt wooden facades, carved and painted and festooned with fabrics, fronted the cave entrances. These caves, as far as we can tell, were not accommodation for monks (who ate and slept in the monasteries in the valley), but places for worship and meditation; none the less the whole scene will still have been a hive of activity, the yellow robes of monks visible everywhere.

Dominating everything, of course, are the carved Buddhas, but in 629 it is not just their size that is astonishing but their colour and adornment as well. Let us hear how Xuanzang describes them:

> To the north-east of the royal city, on the side of the mountain, there is a stone statue of the standing Buddha. It is 140–50 feet high, of a dazzling gold colour and resplendent with ornamentation of precious substances. To the east of it is a monastery built by an earlier king of the country. East of this is a standing image of Shakyamuni Buddha, more than 100 feet high, made of brass, the pieces of which have been cast separately and then assembled to make up the statue.

It is clear enough that Xuanzang is talking about the two famous Buddhas, but in that case his mistake about the smaller Buddha, thinking it was made of brass, is peculiar, and suggests just how rich its decoration was: so much metallic embellishment or such rich colours that this otherwise accurate witness thinks it *is* metal. For the larger statue also his description seems at first sight almost irreconcilable with the image as it was in 2001.

But with some historical research, some cutting-edge science, and a dose of old-fashioned imagination, we can get pretty close to Xuanzang's vision. There are strong indications from other sources that the clothes of both Buddhas were very brightly coloured in the Buddhist period. In the last chapter we heard about the traces of colour still visible on the statues into modern times. But our clearest evidence about the original appearance of the Buddhas comes from a combination of the most up-to-date scientific research and accounts of the statues from Islamic sources after the end of Buddhism in Bamiyan. Islamic writers record that they were commonly known in the Middle Ages as the *Surkh But* and the *Khing But*, the 'Red Idol' and 'Moon-white Idol', the earliest surviving testimony coming from the tenth century, just after the period when we think the last vestiges of Buddhist observance disappeared from Bamiyan and its environs. Those descriptions might at a stretch just indicate the subtly different composition, and hence tint, of the two Buddhas' clay coatings, but work since 2001 on the fragments of the Buddhas has yielded fascinating information about the painting of the statues in the Buddhist period. It transpires that the statues were repeatedly repainted, and that until the very last stage of painting they followed the same colour scheme. In both cases the Buddha's *samghati* or outer cloak was in the first instance painted pink (perhaps as the base for another layer now lost); next it was overpainted a bright orange-red derived from minium or red lead, which apparently rapidly discoloured to black; at which point both Buddhas were repainted white, and the smaller stayed that colour. The larger Buddha subsequently received a final coat of red – which with a bit of natural discoloration left the two statues as they appeared to those early Muslim witnesses, the Red Idol and the Moon-white (or Grey) Idol.

We noted in the first chapter some damage to the larger Buddha's right leg, a clean slice taken from the knee down marked by regular post holes. This has generally been interpreted by archaeologists as an indication of renovations (the application of some kind of wooden armature) after some damage to the lower leg soon after its initial carving. But surely the holes below the right knee, along with the similar holes below the left arm of this Buddha and the even larger holes tracking upwards towards his right arm, indicate how the lower clothing of the statue was realised, the fall of his *samghati* on his left side, and the sweep of the gown up to his right hand – all supported by a system of projecting beams. An image of the Dipankara Buddha (a Buddha believed to have appeared in an era before the 'historical' Buddha, Shakyamuni) found at Mes Ainak, can give us an idea of how the statue's clothing may have looked, paralleling also the outsized heads of both figures and their generally slightly awkward proportions. It goes without saying that a realisation of a comparable image on this entirely incomparable scale would have been stunning – and extremely vulnerable to the regular seismic activity in the Hindu Kush. It is no surprise that only the post holes of this elaborate construction survived into modern times.

The inner lining of the *samghati* on both Buddhas, visible especially under their raised right arms, was painted blue throughout all these repaintings of the outer surface, a pigment made from the lapis lazuli mined at Sar-i Sang in north-eastern Afghanistan: the same pigment, staggeringly from the same source, graced the gowns of many a medieval European Madonna. Visitors in the nineteenth and twentieth centuries had noticed lingering traces of red paint on the

9. A relief of the Dipankara Buddha found at Mes Ainak, a Buddhist site associated with ancient copper workings south-east of Kabul. The posture, clothing and general style of this image can give us an idea of how the larger Buddha at Bamiyan would originally have looked. The specific Buddha depicted here, the Dipankara, is a Buddha who existed in a previous epoch. The figure prostrating himself at the feet of the Buddha is laying his long hair across a puddle for the Buddha to walk upon: far into the future this young man will be reincarnated as the 'historical' Buddha, Shakyamuni, the Buddha of the present epoch.

55m Buddha, and Robert Byron had suggested that the red was ground for a gilt overlay. There were also reports of traces of gold paint on the neck and cheeks of the 38m Buddha, which may help us to imagine how Xuanzang could have interpreted it as a metal statue. But the recent research has not yet found any evidence of gilding.

The jewellery implied in Xuanzang's account may have been hung from the Buddhas' ears, or around their necks, and at other points we must imagine the effect of wooden armatures anchored in the stone: both forearms of the smaller Buddha and the right arm of the larger project out from the rock, and we can see again the *mudras* or symbolic hand gestures that helped to identify the aspect of the Buddha being depicted. The smaller Buddha may have been holding his left hand in *varadamudra* (letting it hang down, palm forward), the gesture of charity and compassion, and his right in *abhaya-mudra* (hand up at chest height, palm outward), a gesture representing the dispelling of fear. The larger Buddha may also have been in *abhayamudra*. There is the intriguing further possibility that the blank faces of the statues, long assumed to be evidence of deliberate iconoclasm, were in fact designed to allow the application of elaborate face masks, perhaps of gilded wood, or wood covered with brass. It has even been suggested that structures behind the shoulders of the larger Buddha may have supported flames rising from his shoulders, possibly identifying it as an image of the Dipankara Buddha.

If we are to imagine the Buddhas as richly, even gaudily painted, they would have set the tone for the rest of Buddhist Bamiyan, which would have been a riot of artificial colour in contrast to the striking but entirely natural colours we see today. Externally the cliffs may have carried paint and brightly coloured fabrics; internally many of the caves were decorated with paintings, most commonly multiple images of buddhas, but also images of stupas, donor-figures, and other religious material within a fairly limited repertoire and palette. There were also sculptures within some caves, and architectural mouldings which produced some rather remarkable imitations of free-standing architecture. The niches of the Buddhas were covered in paintings, among the most impressive of which were the mysterious charioteer above the head of the smaller Buddha, mentioned in the last chapter, and a boldly coloured Buddha or Bodhisattva (a related category of enlightened being; this image was christened the 'beau Bodhisattva' by archaeologists) above the most complete of the seated Buddhas in the three niches between the colossal Buddhas. The monasteries too will have been full of wall paintings and brightly painted sculpture, as recent archaeology has confirmed, and the towering stupas, embellished with sculptures and brightly coloured themselves, will also have been decorated with long, colourful streamers attached to their upper levels. But to the vibrant colours of Buddhist Bamiyan we need to add the activity of throngs of people: pilgrims and merchants in an unimaginable array of costumes alongside the yellow-robed monks, the smell of incense, the noise of prayer and chanting, the drums and cymbals of worshippers bringing their own colourful, precious or pungent offerings to the sacred places, and the conches and gongs which marked the passage of the monastic day. Little of this decoration, needless to say, was for its own sake. Painted, adorned and posed, the Buddhas were characterised and symbolic, albeit in ways about which scholars still debate. Meanwhile, the decoration of monastic buildings had the fundamental aim of drawing attention to the doctrine, like the bell tower of a Christian church or the minaret and muezzin of a mosque.

A FABULOUS THIRD BUDDHA ...

There were many large Buddhas at Bamiyan: in addition to the 55m and 38m standing Buddhas, we have already been introduced to the three seated Buddhas which originally occupied niches in the cliff between their colossal neighbours, and there is also the 7m Buddha in the side valley at Kakrak. In 2008 another giant Buddha was discovered, buried underground roughly halfway between the niches of the colossal statues. This image, discovered by the French-Afghan archaeologist Zemaryalai Tarzi (who has been digging at Bamiyan since 2003), was an example of one of the most compelling iconographical representations of the Buddha, the *parinirvana*. This image traditionally represents the Buddha's passage into final nirvana, lying on his death bed, carefully orientated north–south and reclining on his right side, his hand cushioning his head and his features set in an extraordinarily serene expression of composure in the face of absolute extinction. The Bamiyan *parinirvana* is estimated to have been 19m long. Only fragments of the statue have so far been recovered – its upper right arm, neck and shoulders, and the pillow on which the dying Buddha was resting – but the find was a morale-boosting discovery, seven years after the destruction of the other statues.

Delighted as Professor Tarzi was to have found it, the 19m statue wasn't the one he was actually looking for. The real goal of his search was another *parinirvana* image, one 'announced' to the world media at a press conference in Kabul in 2002 by the publicity-hungry French intellectual Bernard-Henri Lévy, but in fact already well known to anyone who was familiar with Xuanzang's account. For after his description of the two colossal Buddhas, Xuanzang goes on to make electrifying mention of a third: 'Two or three *li* to the east of the city, in a monastery, there is a lying statue of the Buddha entering nirvana, more than 1,000 feet long.' This astonishing claim of a 300m Buddha may gain some slight support from a notice in the sixteenth-century *A'in-i Akbari* by Abu al-Fazl, a detailed account of the administration of the Moghul emperor Akbar, which, after describing the Buddhas at Bamiyan and Kakrak, adds that 'strange to relate, in a cave is placed a coffin which contains the body of one who reposes in his last sleep', or perhaps '… the body of one of the ancient sages who …'. But no sign has ever been found of this super-colossal reclining Buddha, and in that respect Tarzi's efforts, funded by the French government after Lévy's intervention, have so far not borne fruit.

Xuanzang's account of the 1,000-foot Buddha not only grabbed people's attention in 2002 – as Lévy knew it would – but had been doing so for many years, something Lévy omitted to mention. More than one previous visitor had wanted to find a textual error in Xuanzang's account in order to identify the reclining Buddha with a long, low, north–south oriented volcanic formation *west* of Bamiyan known as the Azhdaha or 'Dragon', part of a rich cycle of legends concerning the conversion of Bamiyan to Islam by the great Shi'i hero Hazrat-i Ali, who, as heroes do, slew the dragon, saved the girl and converted the kingdom. It seemed easy to imagine that what was now a Muslim holy site had once been sacred to Buddhists, just as the placement of Islamic *ziarats* or

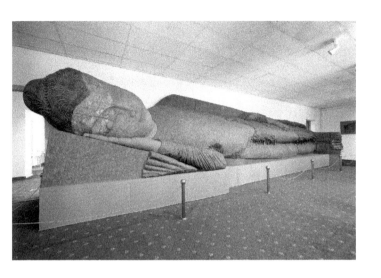

10. The 12m *parinirvana* Buddha (the Buddha on his death bed, at the point of entering ultimate nirvana) in the National Museum of Antiquities of Tajikistan in Dushanbe. The statue was discovered at the important Buddhist site of Ajina-Tepe, excavated in the 1960s and 70s. The 19m *parinirvana* image found at Bamiyan in 2008, and the image seen by Xuanzang, will have shared the same established iconography of the *parinirvana* Buddha, orientated north–south, reclining on his right side, his hand cushioning his head, a serene expression on his face.

shrines at Bamiyan seems often to correspond to the location of the monasteries that preceded them. Unfortunately that appealing idea falls down on a number of counts, and if there is any textual corruption it is much more likely to be in the length Xuanzang attributes to the reclining Buddha. Most authorities think, with regret, that the search for the 1,000-foot Buddha is a wild-goose chase.

... AND A REAL THIRD WONDER

But in the course of *failing* to find Xuanzang's 300m reclining Buddha, Tarzi has discovered a great deal else during his excavations. The 19m reclining Buddha is a case in point, and another of Tarzi's discoveries equally deserves our attention. This is not a statue but a building, but this building will have been, in its day, potentially as awe-inspiring to visitors as the gigantic Buddhas. It will also broaden our understanding of the Buddhist presence in Bamiyan, and help us to grasp the deeper significance of the Buddhas nearby.

In the fields just to the east of the smaller Buddha is the mushroom-shaped ruin we spotted from Shahr-i Gholghola. It is all that remains above ground of a stupa, a lofty structure with a stepped base which was the most important building type in Buddhist architecture. There will have been dozens of stupas across Bamiyan in the Buddhist period, ranging in size from just a few feet high to substantial constructions. *This* stupa, if the archaeologists are interpreting the remains correctly, was (at its greatest extent) quite enormous. Professor Tarzi's excavation of the building has provided us with the full sweep of Bamiyan's history as a Buddhist centre, since it seems the stupa was as old as the Buddhist presence in

11. A reliquary from the fourth or fifth century for the ashes of a revered holy man, found in Pakistan. It is in the shape, somewhat fancifully realised, of a stupa or relic mound, the most important Buddhist building type. The style of stupa represented by this reliquary, and by the Great Stupa at Bamiyan, stands on a continuum between the comparatively plain hemispherical domes of early Indian stupas and the multi-storey towers (pagodas) of the Far East: here the drum and dome recall Indian stupas, while the multiple parasols and the upward elevation anticipate the towering pagoda.

the valley. The earliest levels uncovered by his team go back perhaps as far as the second century AD, and certainly back to a time when the Greek artistic influence very evident in the Buddhist art of those early centuries was present also in the Hindu Kush. This was the so-called 'Gandharan' period when Greek artistic styles, the legacy of Greek kingdoms that followed Alexander's conquests and ongoing trade connections with the Mediterranean, had been applied to Buddhist images. That distant European presence in Afghanistan was, as we shall see in Chapter 4, something later European visitors would be keen to resuscitate: the possibility that Alexander the Great might actually have marched his troops through Bamiyan, a millennium before the creation of the Buddhas (it *is* only a possibility), was a source of great excitement to many Western visitors in the nineteenth century. But by the time the giant Buddhas were carved, Indian influence in the form of Gupta art was reasserting itself, alongside influences from Iran, central Asia and China. Just the faintest echoes of the Greeks persisted in Bamiyan by the time Xuanzang visited in the seventh century, the full, naturalistic folds of the smaller Buddha's monastic cloak, for example (the larger Buddha's V-neck was a Gupta detail), and both Buddhas' naturalistic hair; more strikingly, the Greek lettering in which Xuanzang tells us the local language was still written. One reasonably plausible explanation of the name Hindu Kush, among some very implausible ones, is that it derives from a Greek name for the range, *ho Indikos Kaukasos*, 'the Indian Caucasus'. One ceases to wonder that in this melting pot of melting pots Iranian peoples followed Indian religion and used a Mediterranean writing system.

On the evidence of Tarzi's excavations of this stupa, this

first period of Buddhist worship at Bamiyan, with its Gandharan artefacts, seems to have ended violently in the fifth century: the prime suspects are a fleetingly dominant tribal grouping called the Hephthalites. But the most ambitious development of this stupa belongs to a second, greater period of activity in Bamiyan, which coincides with the developments in the sixth century we considered earlier, the shift in the trade routes, Turkish domination, and the carving of the Buddhas. Ultimately the stupa seems to have burned to the ground, leaving just the core represented by the lump of masonry that survives, though when and whether deliberately or by accident we cannot say, and reconstructing the building is a matter of quantifying and interpreting the amount of burned material remaining at the site. On this basis Tarzi calculates that at its full extent – comprising a square, stepped base, a dome, and an elaborate series of parasols rising to a spire topped with a rainwater dish – the building may have reached a height of 80m. The beauty of Tarzi's archaeology is that it has conjured up a building that answers to accounts that survive in Islamic sources, dating back to the eleventh century at least, of a remarkable building at Bamiyan, 'a sanctuary which towers in the sky with lofty columns', decorated with 'all the birds and all the frightening creatures of the earth'.

Lofty, architecturally elaborate, richly decorated and colourful, no doubt also with huge banners attached to its higher reaches, the Great Stupa at Bamiyan must have been a remarkable sight. The Islamic sources that mention it employ the same awed tone as is used to describe the Buddhas, and that certainly chimes with the status of the stupa in Buddhist ritual. For the stupa was always the primary religious monument of Buddhism, the centre of the monastic community, a cult image and object of worship in itself. Essentially the stupa is a sepulchral mound, a monument representing the crowning moment in the career of the historical Buddha, Shakyamuni, his death and entry into final nirvana at Kushinagara (the moment captured visually in the image of the reclining Buddha). Stupas typically contained holy relics that in some sense embodied the Buddha, physical remnants of the historical Buddha, the Buddha of this era, of Buddhas of the past, or of other holy men, or else artefacts such as a Buddha's begging bowl or sacred texts; at Shotorak (a name meaning 'Little Camel'), north of Kabul, a terracotta vase found in a stupa contained nothing but earth – presumably sacred earth from a holy location. The stupa might just mark some holy spot and contain no relics at all. But insofar as it marks the Buddha's ultimate extinction in any humanly conceivable form, it is the Dharmakaya, the Buddha essence, that the stupa fundamentally represents, a concept of Buddhahood that leaves far behind the historical Buddha, the exceptionally insightful but human teacher. This cosmic Buddha was an embodiment of the Absolute, the principle from which all else in the universe emanates. In its fully developed form, the stupa was a counterpart of the most familiar Buddhist artistic form, the metaphysical cosmic diagram known as the mandala, and like the mandala the stupa was governed by a strict ritual order, oriented to the four points of the compass, expressing the fundamental, all-encompassing nature of the Buddha.

The elaboration of this central Buddhist architectural form as Buddhism spread out of India and towards the Far East is a fascinating case of cultural diffusion. The towering stupa at Bamiyan with its multiple parasols, each one a symbol of royalty and a gesture of respect to the Buddha essence enshrined within it, stood on a continuum between the relatively plain hemispherical domes with minimal upward elevation of early Indian stupas and the narrow, multi-storeyed tower in east Asia known as the pagoda. But in all its forms the building represented the goal of every Buddhist: transcendence of this illusory world of rebirth and suffering. As monks or pilgrims moved clockwise around it (following the path of the sun), stopping periodically to make offerings or chant or meditate, they were drawing themselves closer to that ultimate release. In other words, this stunning building, now a rather unprepossessing lump of rough masonry, was in its most important aspect something much greater than a visual wonder. It was an engine for salvation, a spiritual lighthouse, source of the higher, ineffable illumination that brought enlightenment. As such, the Great Stupa of Bamiyan can help us towards the view of Bamiyan as it might have been experienced by an observant Buddhist in its heyday, the vision hinted at in the Arabic text that talks of a viewer 'seeking [the Buddhas] as an object for his attention with reverence for them.'

The Great Stupa of Bamiyan started for us as a visually striking building to be reconstructed. It has emerged as what it truly was, a means to achieve the Buddhist end of nirvana, or 'snuffing out'. Of course, the aspirations of the worshippers will have been as varied as in any church. Xuanzang gives us this impression of the range of religious observance at Bamiyan:

For the pureness of their faith they far surpass neighbouring

12. The Great Stupa as it is today, a mushroom-shaped piece of masonry in the fields just east of the smaller Buddha. The land excavated by Professor Tarzi's team is essential to the livelihood of the local farmers, and is returned to farmland after every excavation season. Bamiyan's economy today is predominantly agricultural: the quality of its potatoes is particularly celebrated.

kingdoms. From the Three Jewels down to the hundred divinities there is no object of veneration regarding which they do not give proof of sincerity, and to whom they do not deliver with full heart a reverent worship. When the merchants come and go, the gods show them favourable omens; if there are evilly inspired misfortunes, they seek religious merit.

'The Three Jewels' (the Buddha, his Teachings and the Community) is a way of describing orthodox Buddhism, but clearly practices from other religions are also being performed, and archaeology seems to confirm the presence in Bamiyan of Zoroastrians, at least. Meanwhile, it sounds as though the merchants' interest in Buddhism focuses on more immediate concerns: the outcomes of their commercial undertakings rather than liberation from the cycle of rebirth. (Buddhism did enforce a fairly sharp divide between the lay community and the monks.) Nevertheless, Bamiyan was an assertively Buddhist place. Xuanzang also gives us precious evidence of what we might call the 'state religion' of Bamiyan. In connection with the monastery of the '1,000-foot' Buddha, he tells us:

It is in this monastery that the king of the country organises each time the great assembly of the moksha. *Beginning with his wife and his children, he gives them all away; and when the treasure has been given to exhaustion, he gives in addition himself. The ministers and functionaries then approach the priests to buy them back. It is considered essential to act this way.*

A delicate balance of power between the king and the religious establishment is implied here, but the centrality of Buddhism to the life and political administration of the country is clear enough. It follows, then, that if we are to see through this project of imaginatively reconstructing the Buddhas of Bamiyan, we must recreate, not just a scene of intense noise, activity, smell and colour – though it was undoubtedly that – but a landscape of religious significance, a space dedicated to communicating the liberating doctrine of Buddhism. The question becomes, what did the Buddhas of Bamiyan *signify*?

THE IMAGE OF THE BUDDHA

Buddhism is a frantically schismatic religion, the consequence of the Buddha's insistence that there should be no central doctrinal authority after he had gone, although Buddhist schisms were generally quite friendly affairs, at least compared with those occurring in their Western counterparts. Bamiyan was the home of a particular school of Buddhism, the consequence of more than one doctrinal dispute between monks. An impression of the issues at stake can be gained from an account of the first great schism within the Buddhist monastic community, which indirectly brought into being the type of Buddhism practised at Bamiyan, that of the Lokottaravadin school. The disagreement at the heart of this first schism concerns the individual who has achieved enlightenment, the *arhant*, and the degree to which he could be considered perfect. A monk called Mahadeva argued that the *arhant* was in certain respects fallible:

Mahadeva, a monk renowned for his learning and virtue, maintained a group of five propositions according to which the

[72]

*Arhant could be seduced in dream, have doubts, have ignorance
mainly in regard to his quality of Arhant, be led on the Path
of deliverance by another, and pronounce the word 'Suffering!'
while in meditation.*

These may seem footling grounds on which to part
company, but the sect that traced its origins to Mahadeva's
propositions, the Mahasamghikas, and from which the
Lokottaravadins in turn branched off, was an important stage
on the road to the elaborated form of Buddhism known as the
Mahayana, the 'Greater Vehicle' (as opposed to the Hinayana,
'Lesser Vehicle', of early Buddhism). In insisting on the fal-
libility, however slight, of the *arhant*, Mahadeva is opening up
a gap with the higher beings, Buddhas and Bodhisattvas, who
represented perfection for the Mahayana. The Lokottaravadins at Bamiyan were still officially Hinayana, but they were
in an even clearer way forerunners of the Mahayana: *lokottara*
is the Sanskrit for 'supramundane, transcendent', which suggests that the defining doctrines of this school concerned the
supreme transcendence of the Buddha. The doctrinal questions are complex in the extreme, but it comes as no surprise that in this respect, as in others, Bamiyan stood at the
boundary.

Knowing what flavour of Buddhists inhabited the monasteries of Bamiyan can bring us closer to the ultimate question
of this chapter: why was the religion represented here by two
colossal Buddhas? No doubt multiple factors were in play. The
insight that Xuanzang allows us into the king's involvement in
the cult might make us suspect that in Bamiyan, as elsewhere,
supersized statues were designed to reflect the power and
piety of a royal dedicator, like the giant fifth-century Buddhas

at Yungang in China, closely identified with the Northern Wei emperors, or the colossal bronze seated Buddha at Todai-ji monastery in Japan, a commission by the emperor in the eighth century which nearly bankrupted his country. In a comparable way the highly ornamented image of the Buddha that Xuanzang tells us he saw at Bamiyan – apparently festooned with jewellery, a style which seems to have been popular throughout the Hindu Kush – associated the Buddha with royalty and assimilated secular rulers to the Buddha as the Chacravartin, the benign universal ruler. Nevertheless, doctrinal considerations are likely to have been decisive, and it is in the beliefs of the Lokottaravadins that we have the best chance of finding the rationale for giant Buddhas.

Big, small or middling, the fundamental aim of creating an image of the Buddha, like the building of stupas, was to achieve merit, and bring the dedicator and his fellow humans (starting with those close to him) nearer to salvation: a typical inscription beneath a fifth-century statue from Mathura, India, reads: 'This is the pious gift of the Buddhist monk Yasadinna. The merit of this gift, whatever it may be, let it be for the attaining of supreme knowledge by his parents, teachers, preceptors and all living beings.' As the object of contemplation by others, the idealised representation of the Buddha, an image finer than the mundane, with a serenity of expression and gesture suggestive of his transcendence of this illusory world, drew those that contemplated it closer to nirvana. The Buddhas of Bamiyan certainly demanded even more than most Buddha images to be contemplated. But the images of the Buddha at Bamiyan, both in statue form and in the paintings decorating many of the caves, represent a fascinating development in the history of the Buddha image, a remarkable history already by the sixth century. The earliest Buddhist representations portrayed the lives and past lives of the Buddha as models for worshippers, and initially the Buddha himself was represented by symbols (such as footprints, a tree, a wheel, or a stupa), as if a human image, however idealised, could not convey his transcendent state. At around the end of the first century AD, in a momentous development, the Buddha begins to be represented in human form, albeit highly idealised and stylised. Debate continues to rage about the catalyst for this change, the old idea that the Buddha image emerged when the religion encountered Greek traditions of figurative art being less popular now. But for our purposes the important point is that, even as Buddhist art focused in on the figure of the Buddha, there remained a narrative dimension to the image: moments in the Buddha's life often being alluded to in images surrounding the central figure. This Buddha still has an anchor, in other words, albeit increasingly tenuous, in a time and place. But at Bamiyan we have weighed anchor. If we look at the painting from the cupola of a cave at Kakrak, now in the Musée Guimet, Paris, we find a composition which we have to call 'hieratic' or 'iconic' rather than 'narrative'. No attempt is made to give the images of the Buddha depth, and they are unrestricted by any intimation of a temporal or spatial context. This Buddha stands apart, timeless and transcendent, from any version of the sensory world. The plurality of Buddhas in the Kakrak image (an image replicated across Bamiyan) reinforces this principle of timelessness. The older notion of successive Buddhas in successive eras has yielded to the idea of a Buddhahood that is quite beyond time. In this conception of a divine realm of enlightened beings, multiple Buddhas coexist,

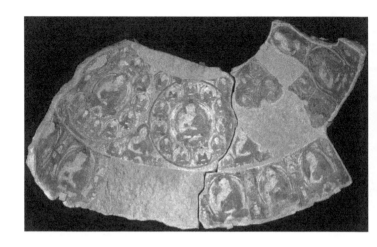

13. Paintings from the ceiling of a cave at Kakrak. The 'iconic' character of
the depiction of the Buddha, and the multiplicity of Buddhas represented,
reflect developments in the conception of Buddhahood. The Buddha in
these paintings is unrestricted by time or space, a universal force: similar
ideas probably informed the carving of the colossal Buddhas. The Buddhas
on the lower level are interspersed with images of stupas, evidence for the
appearance of the Great Stupa at Bamiyan.

although their plurality can always be resolved into a vision of transcendent, harmonious unity, here conveyed by the rings of Buddhas around one central figure. It was thus an image of this diverse universe, which nevertheless achieves unity at the ineffable level represented by essential Buddhahood, that the monks meditating in the cave at Kakrak were contemplating.

The carved Buddhas reflect a similar impulse to isolate this transcendent (*lokottara*), cosmic Buddha; and whatever else contributed to the size of the Buddhas at Bamiyan, this trajectory in Buddhism's conception of its central figure, from exceptional monkish teacher to the guiding presence in the universe, must be the critical factor. The message of Bamiyan to Buddhist worshippers was quite as hyperbolic in its implications as its artistic medium, the colossal, brightly painted and flamboyantly decorated images: they were gazing at the ultimate origin of everything.

The gigantic Buddhas of Bamiyan, it appears, reflected the beliefs of the Lokottaravadin monks whose lives they oversaw. But the scholar Deborah Klimburg-Salter, author of the most detailed study of Buddhist Bamiyan, makes a bold further argument to the effect that the whole complex of Buddhas was designed to represent to the visitor a lesson in three-dimensional form (from a Lokottaravadin viewpoint) on the way to enlightenment. This lesson was perhaps followed by Xuanzang himself, since (according to Huili) he was escorted around Bamiyan by two local monks and seems, from his own account, to have moved in the ritually prescribed, clock-wise direction around the site, from the city at the western end of the valley to the western 55m Buddha, then the 38m Buddha, and so on. Each Buddha, as we have seen, had a path around it at both foot- and head-height, allowing pilgrims to circumambulate in the same clockwise direction, praying and making offerings.

According to Klimburg-Salter, Xuanzang's itinerary around Bamiyan, bearing in mind the context of a trend in Buddhist belief and art from the Buddha's historical career towards his spiritual career, might be understood in a similar way to the remarkably intricate Borobudur monument on Java, which has been described as 'a psychophysical pilgrim's path: the terraces lead the pilgrim through the different cosmic spheres, levels of apprehension, and stages of redemption. It is an initiation course into the Buddhist faith, executed in stone', leading the pilgrim symbolically through the consecutive levels of the Mahayana universe. Now every Buddhist artefact is geared to the aims of the religion, an aid to transcendence, but if Klimburg-Salter is right, a walk along the Bamiyan cliff would take one through a kind of spiritual biography of Shakyamuni: the 55m Buddha would be a previous embodiment of the Buddha known as the Dipankara Buddha; the 38m Buddha would be Shakyamuni on the point of being incarnated as the 'historical' Buddha; and the great reclining Buddha mentioned by Xuanzang, whatever size it really was, being Shakyamuni after enlightenment and the establishment of the all-important monastic community.

This is an ingenious and attractive theory. The idea of such a coherent spiritual message perhaps invests too much in the assumption of simultaneous construction of the monuments of Bamiyan, which is not wholly supported by radiocarbon dating, and our understanding of the topography of Buddhist Bamiyan, as we have seen, is less concrete than Klimburg-Salter's theory ideally requires. Fundamentally, the question of the design of the Buddhist community at Bamiyan – did it develop organically, or was it the realisation of a dynastic master plan? – still resists any conclusive answer. The colossal Buddhas themselves could be the result of anything from a king's bold assertion of his creed and wealth to competition between monasteries – building the larger Buddha after the comparatively smaller one further down the valley might just, at a stretch, have been a monastic version of keeping up with the Joneses. In the absence of clearer evidence from the sixth and seventh centuries, these are imponderables. Nevertheless, Klimburg-Salter's essential idea is a profound and convincing one – that the most authentic view of the monuments of Bamiyan is that which reads into them the message of salvation from suffering promoted by the Lokottaravadin school of Bamiyan.

Like many religions, Buddhism has always experienced a tension between its doctrines and its artistic representations. Those early aniconic representations of the Buddha, although they are still not fully understood by modern scholars, seem to reflect a sense that the Buddha's enlightened state places him beyond conventional modes of depiction. When (highly idealised) portraits of the Buddha did emerge, and then colossal statues at Bamiyan and elsewhere, they were all still trying to meet the tricky specification of an image conveying something that was by definition beyond expression or sense-based understanding. Of course, it is paradoxical challenges like this that have generated some of the greatest works of religious art, Islamic calligraphy or a Shaker chair ('made by someone capable of believing that an angel might come and sit on it', in the words of Thomas Merton). But to the true adept an image of the Buddha can only ever be a means to a much higher end, evoking an intuition of a higher existence in the worshipper's mind, and it follows that the most effective image will render itself superfluous as it stimulates the meditating viewer to grasp the emptiness of this phenomenal realm and all its contents. We might say that the Buddha image, while essential to Buddhist worship, is only truly efficacious when it is appreciated to be no image at all, a solid object paradoxically pushing us towards nothingness.

In this rarefied space we have completed a kind of circle, refilling those gaping, empty niches at Bamiyan only to learn that an enlightened observer, gazing at the images from across the valley, would know that even the tallest, most colourful, most extravagantly decorated Buddha was mere empty illusion. When Bamiyan was Buddhist, in other words, the Buddhas of Bamiyan were at their most wonderful, but also their least.

3

....

ISLAM CONTEMPLATES
THE BUDDHAS

One cannot believe that these were made by human hands.
Mahmud ibn Wali of Balkh, *Bahr al-Asrar*

The men who ordered the destruction of the Bamiyan
Buddhas in 2001 claimed it as an impeccably Islamic act.
The statues were idols; Islam repudiated idol-worship; their
demolition was thus the duty of any true Muslim. Many
Muslims disagreed, including that delegation of senior
Islamic scholars, led by Yusuf al-Qaradawi (not exactly a
liberal himself), who travelled to Qandahar to try to persuade Mullah Omar not to pursue a course of action that
(the scholars insisted) was contrary to Islamic law. Nevertheless, many Muslims were instinctively approving of an action
that resonated with certain undeniable themes in Islamic
history and thought. A celebratory calendar produced by
the fundamentalist Al-Rashid Trust, with images of the
process of destruction, was to be seen all over Pakistan in
2001, for example, and if Al-Qa'ida were as close to events
as some suspect, that is exactly what we would expect. The
greatest talent of bin Laden and his associates has always
been to harness the instinctive, unthinking sympathy of a

constituency much wider than the narrow hard core of militant Islamists.

Yet for all Al-Qa'ida's skill in marketing its ideology, it remains the case that the version of Islam it promotes is an exceptionally restricted one – indeed, what the fundamentalism of the Taliban and Al-Qa'ida had in common (alongside much they did not) was an uncompromising insistence that their extremely reductive readings of Islam were the only way to practise the faith, implicitly and explicitly condemning as heretical much of the rich breadth of beliefs and practices that make up Islamic observance and culture today and have done throughout its history. In relation to Bamiyan, an opposition to idol worship is without question a significant thread in Islamic thought (as it is in other religions), but at the same time Bamiyan itself betrays the realities of the Islamic commitment to iconoclasm: Bamiyan has been Islamic now for about 1,200 years, 1,200 years of complex, dramatic, often violent geopolitics, and 1,200 years for the vast majority of which the Buddhas sustained *no significant damage*. The task of this chapter will be to investigate in detail how these colossal idols fared in the new religious environment ushered in by the Arab invasions of the seventh and eighth centuries, and with luck two messages in particular will emerge. Firstly, that it is nonsensical to boil down the wide spectrum of responses to the Buddhas by Muslims from the eighth century to the twenty-first to any single, monolithic 'Islamic' view, let alone to a rigid religious imperative to destroy them. And secondly, without ever downplaying Islam's inherent distaste for religious images, that it is in the Islamic period that the Buddhas enjoy their second, great period of celebrity – indeed, there is no time at which Bamiyan is more clearly and unequivocally treated as a Wonder than this.

The history of Bamiyan doesn't get any simpler (or less fascinating) after Islam is established: we have a millennium of history to cover, and this is *Afghan* history, history as it happens at a cultural and political crossroads. We need to consider how Bamiyan was converted to Islam in the first place (a more gradual and subtle process than one might assume), and then the intense curiosity that the new Islamic world felt for the non-Islamic cultures it found at its eastern fringe. The vestiges of Buddhism, and the Buddhas of Bamiyan especially, were the focus of great interest. We shall see how that interest was fuelled by an influential family, the Barmakids, which traced its origins to the great Buddhist centre of Balkh, north of the Hindu Kush, but which achieved power and prominence under the Abbasid caliphate, the last dynasty to maintain control of the vast empire, extending from North Africa to Afghanistan, conquered by the Arabs in the dramatic first century of Islam. The Abbasid caliphs, for example Harun al-Rashid (now best known, like the Barmakids, from the *Arabian Nights*), ruled this Arab empire from Baghdad in the eighth and ninth centuries. But central control of such a far-flung empire was never going to last long, and we shall also investigate some of the local dynasties that sprang up as the power of the caliphs in Baghdad declined and the empire fragmented: in particular, two empires based in Afghanistan from the tenth to the thirteenth centuries, the Ghaznavids (including the notorious 'breaker of idols' Mahmud of Ghazni), and the Ghurids (who made Bamiyan one of their major centres). That part of Bamiyan's story ends decisively in 1221, when Genghis Khan obliterated the city. But Bamiyan does not disappear from history: a new people settle the valley, and tell their own stories to explain its remarkable monuments. Meanwhile other empires rise and fall, most notably the Moghul Empire in India, which at its greatest extent included much of Afghanistan.

TWO UNTYPICAL MUSLIMS

But let me begin by giving my fundamental point – that the typical Islamic response to the Buddhas is entirely untypical – a face. Two faces, in fact, those of two of the most important men to feature in this book, along with their autobiographies: Abdul Ghaffar Khan, author of *My Life and Struggle*; and the adventurer Babur, who founded the Moghul Empire and in his autobiography, the *Baburnama*, described his rise to power in a remarkably intimate form that still speaks vividly to readers 500 years after its composition.

Abdul Ghaffar Khan (1890–1988), also known as the 'Frontier Gandhi', was a proud Pashtun, a member of the ethnic group which, as well as being the largest in Afghanistan, also dominates the north-west of Pakistan. A relic of the British Raj, the Durand Line, marks the border between Afghanistan and Pakistan – and divides the Pashtuns down the middle, a lingering source of resentment. Ghaffar Khan was born on the eastern side of that line, in what was British India (and later Pakistan), but it was not a frontier that the Frontier Gandhi ever recognised. A devout Muslim and a supporter and confidant of Mahatma Gandhi (and like Gandhi committed to strictly non-violent methods), Ghaffar Khan devoted his long life to three great causes: the independence of India from British rule, the creation of a unified India shared by Hindus and Muslims, and self-determination for his own people, the Pashtuns, now divided between Pakistan and Afghanistan.

14. Abdul Ghaffar Khan (the 'Frontier Gandhi') with Gandhi at a pro-independence meeting in Peshawar, 17 May, 1938. Ghaffar Khan allied his Pashtun independence movement, the 'Red Shirts', with Gandhi's Indian National Congress, and he campaigned with Gandhi for a unified India shared by Hindus and Muslims. His movement was sidelined as pressure increased for a separate Muslim state after independence. Subsequently Ghaffar Khan spent even more time in prison under the Pakistani authorities than he had under the British.

Had his peaceful, pluralist vision been realised, the situation in India, Pakistan and Afghanistan (currently the most volatile region in the world), would certainly be very different, but as his obituary in the *New York Times* put it, 'The only goal he attained was the first'. India achieved independence, but was partitioned along religious lines, amid terrible bloodshed, into India and Pakistan. Ghaffar Khan's subsequent efforts to achieve a degree of Pashtun autonomy within Pakistan and Afghanistan met with no greater success, but did ensure that he spent even more time in prison under the new Pakistani authorities than he had under the British. Ghaffar Khan was buried, in a pointed gesture, not on the Pakistani side of the border but in Jalalabad, Afghanistan.

The attitude to the Buddhas of Bamiyan of two deeply religious Pashtuns, Ghaffar Khan and Mullah Omar, could hardly contrast more. In his autobiography Ghaffar Khan regrets that 'our country' (the imagined country of the united Pashtuns, 'Pashtunistan') 'which, at different periods of history, was the cradle of learning and culture could, under unfavourable circumstances, and because of the ignorance of the *mullahs*, sink into a state where there was no room left for such good work as education and learning'. (These prophetic words were written in the 1960s.) The archaeological vestiges of Buddhism in Pakistan and Afghanistan he takes as evidence of these past moments of cultural achievement, to which present-day Pashtuns should aspire, and chief among them is Bamiyan, where 'even today two magnificent statues of Gautama the Buddha can be seen', which are 'probably the largest statues of Buddha in the world' and 'an unparalleled example of perfection in the art of sculpture'.

A great man, undoubtedly, but was Ghaffar Khan

representative of any broader trend in Muslim thinking? It is rather doubtful, and certainly among Pashtuns his liberal social ideas – a radical commitment to women's rights, for example – were not universally shared. (For that matter, a pacifist Pashtun is a very rare bird indeed.) Our second example, Babur, may look more promising for those, Muslims and non-Muslims, who like to see iconoclasm as somehow hard-wired into Islam, and who thus believe the destruction of the Buddhas had been due since the establishment of Islam. But a closer look will reveal Babur to be no more typical than Ghaffar Khan.

Babur visited Bamiyan on repeated occasions in his early career, and indeed experienced one of the most perilous moments of his life (which makes for one of the most dramatic passages of the *Baburnama*) in the mountains nearby. It was the winter of 1506–7, and Babur had been visiting his cousins at their court in Herat, the city in western Afghanistan which was at the time the greatest cultural centre of the Islamic world. Babur found himself awkward and out of place among his sophisticated and hard-drinking relatives: 'Although these princes were outstanding in the social graces,' he comments, 'they were strangers to the reality of military command and the rough and tumble of battle.' He decided to return immediately to Kabul, even though it was midwinter, and to take the central route through the Hindu Kush. In no time Babur and his companions were in serious trouble: 'That day there was an amazing snowstorm. It was so terrible we all thought we were going to die … By the time of the night prayer the snowstorm was still raging so much that I sat all huddled up. Four spans of snow were on my back and covering my head and ears. My ears got frostbite.'

Babur was experiencing, as others had before, the brutality of winter in the Hindu Kush. Xuanzang had also suffered terrible conditions crossing the mountains from Balkh, and the great traveller Ibn Battuta connected the appalling weather he endured to the name of the mountain range: 'Hindu Kush' means 'Killer of Hindus', he claims, 'because the slaves brought from India die in great numbers in these mountains from the extreme cold and the quantity of snow'. For Babur, at last, the snow abated, and he and his men struggled on towards Yakaolang, west of Bamiyan, where they found food and warm lodgings.

Although Babur passed through the Bamiyan valley on other occasions too, and knew it very well (we heard him in the last chapter speaking of the four rivers in the vicinity of Bamiyan from which it is possible to drink in a single day), it is a striking fact that his account never once mentions the Buddhas. When Rory Stewart followed the central route in 2002, occasionally guided by the *Baburnama* and accompanied by a huge dog he had named Babur, he encountered apathy about the Buddhas from people he spoke to in Bamiyan, and drew a parallel with Babur's apparent unconcern for the pre-Islamic past. This lack of interest (from Babur *and* the locals, it seems) 'may reflect the Islamic opposition to pagan idols', Stewart suggests. Earlier Western visitors shared the assumption that the Buddhas must have been offensive to Islamic sentiment, or at any rate that is certainly the implication of the (contradictory) stories relating to damage inflicted on the Buddhas that we find in early British accounts. The antiquarian Charles Masson (actually a deserter from the British army by the name of James Lewis), who visited Bamiyan in 1832, is here referring in the first instance to the Buddhas' absent faces (which may or may not have been deliberately removed, as we have seen). He expresses some scepticism, but accepts the basic premise that the Buddhas were liable to fall victim to Muslim religious objections (Genghis Khan is the only non-Muslim mentioned here):

> *The work of mutilation was one of some labor, and having been executed with precision, will have been directed by authority, possibly by that of the Arabian conquerors. A subsequent and less systematic mutilation has been practised on the idols, by breaking off their hands, and fracturing their legs, for the merits of which Jenghiz, Timur, Aurangzeb, and even Timur Shah Durrani, who are all accused, may dispute.*

There undoubtedly were religiously motivated attacks on the Buddhas before 2001. George Lawrence, one of the British captives taken to Bamiyan in 1842, later recalled some of his Afghan guards firing at the statues as they passed, 'cursing them as idols', and some of the damage to painted or sculpted images of the Buddha within the caves was clearly deliberate. Nevertheless erosion, earthquake and the kind of active neglect illustrated by the use of paintings in the Buddha niches for rifle practice (and before that archery practice: iron arrow-heads were found lodged in the ceiling during restoration) have historically been the more significant villains.

Even Babur's lack of interest in idols looks less doctrinaire when we delve into it further. Later in the *Baburnama* he describes a tour he made of Gwalior, the great Indian fortress city, in the course of which he visited the site of some rock-cut Jain statues, 'shown stark naked with all their private parts exposed'. In other ways the place appealed to Babur, a man deeply committed to formal gardens and who never lost an opportunity to establish or improve one:

> *Around the two large reservoirs inside Urwahi have been dug twenty to twenty-five wells, from which water is drawn to irrigate the vegetation, flowers and trees planted there. Urwahi is not a bad place. In fact, it is rather nice. Its one drawback was the idols, so I ordered them destroyed.*

In fact Babur seems to have limited himself to defacing the statues at Gwalior, and while there is an obvious religious tinge to such an action, it is hard to separate out religious and merely aesthetic motivations here. Elsewhere Babur talks of a garden in the beauty spot of Istalif, north-west of Kabul, which contained a mill stream: 'The stream used to run higgledy-piggledy until I ordered it to be straightened. Now it is a beautiful place.' He concludes an account of a garden he had constructed at Agra, 'Thus, in unpleasant and inharmonious India, marvellously regular and geometric gardens were introduced.' What we are looking at is undoubtedly a strong, religiously inflected aesthetic, but Babur's objection to meandering streams or nude statues could hardly be described as fanaticism. Any religious motivation is so deeply buried in Babur's artistic taste for symmetricality, and so bound up with a central Asian's response to the culture of India (as well as a Muslim's response to Indian religions), that even in an apparently clear-cut case like Gwalior Babur was driven only in part by iconoclastic zeal. The very next day, as he continues his tour, Babur mentions without further comment idols in the temples of Gwalior. As for the Buddhas of Bamiyan, it is as if Babur's rigid aesthetic makes him simply blind to them.

15. A sixteenth-century Moghul illustration, from an illuminated copy of the *Baburnama*, of Babur straightening a higgledy-piggledy mill stream at Istalif, a beauty spot north of Kabul. Babur, the first Moghul emperor, liked nothing better than laying out gardens, and he had firm ideas as to how a garden should look: a regular, symmetrical *chaharbagh* ('four-square garden') which had no place for the 'natural' features essential to Western gardens since Capability Brown.

The truth about Islam and iconoclasm is that many religions harbour concerns about figural representations – even the religion that created the Buddhas of Bamiyan was ambivalent about the portrayal of enlightened beings. And this is particularly true of the Abrahamic religions – Judaism, Islam and Christianity – each of which carries in its scriptures or traditions all the necessary ingredients for a campaign of idol-smashing. History is the witness of that. If anything, the impulse against representation is stronger in Judaism and Christianity since they have in common the authority and uncompromising language of the Second Commandment, for which there is no equivalent in Islam. The closest Islam comes to that scriptural prohibition on 'any graven image, or any likeness of any thing that is in heaven above, or that is in the earth beneath, or that is in the water under the earth' are objections in the Hadith (authoritative traditions conveying the opinions of the Prophet Muhammad) to images of living creatures, both as usurping the creative prerogatives of God and as idolatry (setting up false gods to rival God), and these have been enough to ensure what has been called a 'lingering unease' with such representation in the Islamic world. At the same time, this generalised disapproval of idolatry at the level of principle leaves a lot of room for tolerance of un-Islamic images in practice. In actual fact, Muslim attitudes to the Buddhas often went far beyond polite tolerance, as we shall see, and became something much closer to an assimilation or adoption of these originally Buddhist monuments as remarkable phenomena embodying the mysterious and generous dispensation of the Islamic God. The actions of Mullah Omar and his associates in 2001 are revealed as a product of specific circumstances, not an expression of something essential to Islam. The examples of Ghaffar Khan and Babur suggest it is much more a matter of idiosyncrasy than ideology. Overall, the meeting of Buddhism and Islam at Bamiyan is gratifyingly untidy and undogmatic. But for a proper sense of the overwhelmingly peaceful and creative coexistence of Islam with these relics of an earlier religious culture, we need to appreciate the historical subtleties of the period between Xuanzang's visit to Bamiyan and its emergence as a fully Islamicised community.

THE CONVERSION OF BAMIYAN

The short story is that it took a surprisingly long time for Buddhism to disappear from Bamiyan, and indeed that across the Hindu Kush during the first centuries of the Islamic era (traditionally dating from the Prophet Muhammad's flight to Medina in AD 622) there was something of an explosion of non-Islamic artistic and economic activity. The full story is like any extended account of this strategic geographical space – complicated. If we were to give equal weight to all the sources, for example, we would conclude that Bamiyan was converted to Islam at least three separate times, not counting the conversions effected directly, according to local folklore, by Hazrat-i Ali, son-in-law of the Prophet. A few preliminary explanations of this historical confusion may suggest themselves: simple historical inaccuracy; Bamiyan's perennial talent for telling overlords what they wanted to hear while effectively maintaining its autonomy (already the case at the time of Puluo in 718, we suspected); the natural tendency of warlords to claim a shabby raid for plunder as a triumph for Islam; and above all the fundamental reality of conversion and

Islamisation, which was a gradual, uneven process very unlike the dramatic once-and-for-all transformations favoured by commanders and storytellers alike. As historical boundary markers we may use at one end the time of Xuanzang's visit in the early seventh century, when Bamiyan was a thriving Buddhist centre; and at the other end a clutch of letters in Persian found by French archaeologists which date to about 1211 (thus just a decade before Genghis Khan's devastating visit), by which time Bamiyan seems thoroughly Islamic: 'Daily and nightly, with heart roasted and eyes full of tears, I pray to the Almighty to let me reach the service of happiness with My Master. Let my prayer receive its fulfilment.' What happened in between?

When Xuanzang visited the valley c.629, it was only year 8 or so of the Islamic calendar and any threat to the survival of Buddhism originating in Arabia a thousand miles to the West was unimaginable. But by the time this traveller passed back through Afghanistan after his extended stay in India, in about 645, it was an intriguingly pivotal moment in Asian history. Quite unbeknownst to Xuanzang, the career of the Prophet Muhammad had set off a chain of events which would in the fullness of time overturn the balance of power in central Asia, and transform the culture of Bamiyan. Arab forces had expanded rapidly out of the Arabian peninsula, pushing back the Byzantine Empire to the north and overwhelming the Persian Empire to the east. Control of Persia (Iran) brought the Muslim forces to the edge of what is now Afghanistan, and Arab soldiers first set foot there as early as the mid-seventh century, perhaps just a decade after Xuanzang's departure to the East, and just two decades after the Prophet's death at Medina. But Islam didn't supplant Buddhism at Bamiyan for some considerable time after that. Another Buddhist monk, Hyecho – whose narrative of his travels from China to India was rediscovered only last century – visited Bamiyan in about 727, and still found there 'many monasteries and monks': 'the king, the chiefs and the common people highly revere the Three Jewels'. Over the mountains at Balkh, Hyecho found a more complicated situation: there also 'the king, the chiefs, and the common people' were still devoted to Buddhism, but now 'the place is guarded and oppressed by Arab forces'. The sheer logistics of conquering the difficult, highland territory of Afghanistan are part of the picture here, but only part. An equally important reason for the time it took Islam to become established in Bamiyan is that, as we shall see, conquest by Islamic forces didn't automatically equate to conversion to Islam.

Another document from this period, this time discovered in the last twenty years, illustrates how gradual a process the conversion of the Hindu Kush was. This is one of a remarkable cache of texts in the Bactrian language (written in Greek script) which apparently originated in the royal archives of a principality called Rob, adjacent to Bamiyan. This particular document is a contract for the purchase of an estate, written on leather. It talks of Arab taxation and Arab dirhams as the standard currency (although using the Greek word 'drachma', from which 'dirham' derives), and employs an interesting catch-all legal phrase describing those who must respect this contract, 'men of Rob or men of Bamiyan or Turks or Arabs, or locals, or anyone else'. The Arab invaders are a tangible presence in this contract, but Islam isn't. The only god mentioned is Wakhsh, god of the River Oxus, who is addressed as a witness of the contract, and although a variety of religious practices are hinted at in the document, including some observed in Buddhism and Zoroastrianism, the only oblique reference to Islam is in the Arab method of taxation. That tax, however, may be the most informative detail in the document, because what is being described is the *jizya*, the poll-tax paid by non-Muslims to ensure recognition by their new Arab rulers as *ahl al-dhimma*, 'protected subjects', who were guaranteed an essential freedom of worship. The general military picture we get of this period in Afghanistan is an ongoing struggle between Turks and Arabs for control of the trade routes towards India – in which, needless to say, Bamiyan represented a prize of special value. The future undoubtedly belonged to the Arabs (at the Battle of Talas in 751 they effectively ended Chinese influence in central Asia, for example), and later documents from the Rob archive swap Bactrian for Arabic. But for the moment the struggle was far from one-sided, and the more important thing that we learn from the Bactrian text – and indeed from Hyecho's report from Balkh, for that matter – is that even when Muslim armies were in charge, their new subjects were free to follow faiths other than Islam.

The northern plains of Afghanistan were finally conquered by the end of the eighth century, but it was three or even four centuries after its first arrival in Afghanistan before the eastern parts of the country embraced Islam (and in the more remote parts, that process wasn't completed until the nineteenth century). This is partly because of effective resistance, but it is also a reflection of the invaders' priorities. These were no holy wars, and the guiding aim of the campaigns was not the conversion of non-Muslims, but more mundane considerations such as increased power and wealth. The *jizya* noted in the Bactrian document was part of a sophisticated system for accommodating non-Islamic subjects which the Arabs had developed in connection with the other 'Abrahamic' religions, and later extended to Zoroastrians, Buddhists, Hindus and others, an official, if taxable, tolerance of religious difference (converts to Islam were, of course, exempt). For all who paid, there was no official impediment to free worship, although there were less tangible incentives to convert. What this means, among other things, is that any claims of one-off, lightning-bolt conversions of whole communities, the entire population of Bamiyan for example, are a misrepresentation of a much longer – and much more interesting – process.

The evidence from written sources that comes down to us about the conversion of Bamiyan is contradictory, to the extent that even a single author, Ya'qubi, gives different dates for the conversion of the *shir* or ruler of the principality of Bamiyan in his *History*, in which he claims it happened during the reign of the Abbasid Caliph Al-Mahdi (775–85), and his *Geography*, in which he places it under Al-Mahdi's predecessor Al-Mansur (754–75). This second notice by Ya'qubi comes with some quite interesting detail, including a later *shir* of Bamiyan taking orders from a member of a powerful family of Abbasid officials in Baghdad, the Barmakids, of whom we shall be hearing more soon. But if we scroll forward a full century, Bamiyan still sounds as if it's Buddhist: in about 870 the strongman Ya'qub ibn Laith al-Saffar ('the Coppersmith') captured Bamiyan and, at least according to one way of juggling the sources, sent 'fifty idols of gold and silver' from Bamiyan to Baghdad. That has suggested to some scholars a satisfactorily vivid and conclusive end to Buddhist observance at Bamiyan, but in fact it isn't at all certain that those 'idols' came from Bamiyan rather than a number of other undoubtedly un-Islamic locations that Ya'qub had invaded. At least one more moment of conversion is mentioned in the sources, and this is nearly a century later again: the hero this time is Sebuktigin, the architect of the Ghaznavid Empire, in the second half of the tenth century.

Meanwhile the archaeological evidence from Bamiyan points to a more gradual process of conversion, giving the strong impression that Buddhists must have lived alongside Muslims in the valley for some time: radiocarbon dating of the wall paintings at Bamiyan by Japanese scientists has indicated that Buddhist art continued to be created in the main valley of Bamiyan and in the side valleys well into the ninth century, which suggests that observance may have persisted longest at the remoter locations of Kakrak and Fuladi, up to and even into the tenth century. Another century or more again, and in a surviving document from Bamiyan dated to 1078 we find indications that the Islamisation of Bamiyan was still in some respects rather superficial. This is a kind of prenuptial agreement between Ilyas ibn Shah ibn Mansur and Sharnaz bint Su'luk ibn Abu Nasr, in which a patina of Islamic law masks what seem to be authentically pre-Islamic wedding customs. A local official is mentioned in this document who still seems to carry the title of 'monastery keeper'! There is no doubt that the happy parties to this agreement are Muslim by any reasonable definition, but the boundary between their Islamic present and pre-Islamic past is an intriguingly porous one. In a sense that is no surprise: study of mural painting from the eleventh century at the Ghaznavid palaces along the Helmand river at Lashkari Bazar reveals how much continuity there was between pre-Islamic artistic traditions in Afghanistan and the Islamic art of the Ghaznavid Empire. In addition, as we shall soon see, there are clear indications that Buddhist practices lasted long enough alongside Islamic observance for some of the most informative accounts of Buddhist Bamiyan to be provided by Arabic sources.

Clearly, the model of one-off conversion-by-conquest is not going to help us in Bamiyan, and fortunately a much better way of thinking about the process is available to us. The historian Derryl MacLean has studied the patterns of conversion that followed the eighth-century Arab conquest of Sind, an area corresponding to most of present-day Pakistan which was (prior to the Arab invasion) divided between Hindus and Buddhists. One of his most interesting findings is that the Buddhists of Sind were more sympathetic to the initial Arab invasion than the Hindu population, and also, after the Arab conquest, much more likely to convert to Islam than Hindus, the proof of the pudding being the speed with which Buddhism subsequently disappeared from Sind. The critical difference between the Buddhists and Hindus of Sind, MacLean explains, is something we have considered already in relation to the location of Bamiyan. Buddhism was a thoroughly commercial religion, with a deep, even symbiotic relationship with trade. Monasteries tracked trade routes, and these monasteries were themselves sophisticated commercial operations, servicing passing caravans but also making loans to merchants or organising money-transfers, or even managing industrial operations like the copper mines at Mes Ainak. Buddhism and the mercantile class evidently saw in each other, rootless and itinerant, something essentially sympathetic. In Sind it was their overriding concern for commerce which apparently led the merchants and artisans of the Buddhist communities to support the Arabs against Hindu rulers whose power was feudal and rooted in the countryside, and who were typically unsympathetic to trade.

But those very same commercial interests were Buddhism's downfall. After the Arab conquest the Buddhists of Sind (and later of Bamiyan) had freedom of worship, and with Arab domination also came a hugely expanded world of international trade, any merchant's wildest dream. But Muslim control introduced a religion with a commercial instinct just as sharp as Buddhism's: if Buddhists could trace their mercantile prowess to Tapussa and Bhallika, the merchants who were the Buddha's first disciples, Muslims could trace it to the Prophet himself. So while the huge Arab empire boosted trade, it was trade dominated by Muslim merchants, and trade that bypassed the old engines of international commerce, the Buddhist monasteries. For all Islam's remarkable tolerance of other religions, non-Muslims were second-class citizens in this new Arab world, affected by differential customs rates, for example, and the *jizya* was not negligible, cited by one of the parties to that Bactrian contract as one reason for selling. Consequently the Buddhist mercantile class felt an irresistible draw towards Islam, aside from any inherent appeal of the new religion, as they watched themselves fall further and further away from the prosperity they had formerly enjoyed, and that their Muslim competitors still enjoyed.

The impulse to convert may not have found expression in either religious or economic terms: the old Buddhist elite would simply have seen their social status inexorably eroding, and over time – generations potentially – the old religion would have been progressively abandoned as its adherents aspired to the greater prosperity and status of their Muslim neighbours. To put it simply, to be a successful player in the inter-regional trade that was the life blood of Bamiyan after the eighth century, you had to be Muslim. Such a scenario makes perfect sense of archaeological indications that the Buddhist establishments at sites like Hadda and Ghazni in Afghanistan and Ajina-Tepe in Tajikistan fell into decay rather than being violently overthrown: as I said earlier, these were no holy wars. It also makes sense of some at least of the contradictory indications in the written sources about Bamiyan. Buddhism here was not put to the sword in one dramatic gesture, but dwindled, persisting in the side valleys and in moribund official titles (the king also retained for a while his old title of *shir*), in crumbling mud-brick monastic constructions and, of course, in something that was resistant even to the inexorable laws of socio-economics: the stone-carved Buddhas. It certainly persisted for long enough to find witnesses who would describe their impressions in Arabic, and it is no surprise either that the victory of Islam has traditionally been attributed to triumphant generals or indeed to Hazrat-i Ali brandishing his sabre Zulfiqar, rather than the banal and unromantic motives of self-advancement from which, in reality, it fundamentally resulted.

To Hazrat-i Ali we shall return, but we should quickly fill in events up until the arrival of the Mongols in the thirteenth century. It would seem that during this period of gradual Islamisation, the city of Bamiyan shifted its location, becoming centred on a citadel at Shahr-i Gholghola, from where we contemplated Buddhist Bamiyan in the previous chapter, and that relocation may of course indicate an attempt at some point to mark a formal break with Bamiyan's pre-Islamic

16. Shahr-i Gholghola, the Islamic-era citadel of Bamiyan, pictured from the west. It seems to have enjoyed its greatest period of development in the century or so preceding the destruction of Bamiyan by Genghis Khan in 1221. By 2001 the site was littered with mines and ordnance, and it has been systematically cleared and made safe by the ATC demining agency, in a project coordinated by the Mine Action Coordination Centre of Afghanistan (MACCA), overseen by UNESCO, and funded by the government of Japan.

past. The scattered references to Bamiyan in the following years perhaps indicate a period of comparative decline from the ninth to the eleventh centuries, hardly surprising if the old monastic establishment underpinning the economy had disappeared: a kind of ninth-century gazetteer of the realms of the Abbasid caliphate, written by a man who combined the roles of Postmaster General and Spymaster General, Ibn Khordadba, assessed the tax yield of Bamiyan at the modest sum of 5,000 dirhams. But at the same time the name of one of the four gates of the great entrepôt of Ghazni, the Gate of Bamiyan, implies its continuing commercial relevance. In the latter half of the twelfth century Bamiyan achieved some serious significance again under the Ghurid Empire. The Ghurids had their centre at one of the most romantic locations in Afghanistan, Firuzkuh, 'Turquoise Mountain', in its heyday probably a tent city at the place now occupied by the famous Minaret of Jam, deep in the mountains of Ghur between Bamiyan and Herat. Bamiyan was given to a cadet branch of the Ghurid royal family, and ruled its own empire stretching north beyond the Oxus. But it was only a brief renaissance. In-fighting between the Ghurid princes allowed a power based to the north-east, the Khwarazmian Empire, to supplant the Ghurids in Bamiyan. The Khwarazmians in turn enjoyed their possession of northern Afghanistan for all of the five years or so that take us up to the ominous date of 1221, and the coming of Genghis.

ISLAM VIEWS BAMIYAN

We have just surveyed five centuries of Bamiyan history in about as many paragraphs. But it was in this period also that an Islamic sensibility first encountered, and tried to make sense of, the Buddhas of Bamiyan. And essential to the story of the Islamic response to the Buddhas are the family of the Barmakids, the most successful examples of Buddhists escaping socio-economic decline by embracing Islam. The Barmakids are a famous family in Islamic history, powerful figures under the early Abbasid caliphate in Baghdad in the eighth and ninth centuries, who also made an immense contribution to the development of Islamic intellectual culture. Their contribution is perfectly encapsulated in the tradition that they introduced the manufacture of paper to Baghdad for the first time: this mastery of the technology of paper (allegedly captured from the Chinese at the Battle of Talas in 751) underpinned the dynamic intellectual life of Baghdad and the Islamic empire the Caliphs ruled from that city. First and foremost, however, the Barmakids were administrators. The first ten years of the reign of the most famous Abbasid caliph, Harun al-Rashid, have been described as 'the decade of the Barmakids' (786–96), the climax of the family's power, when Yahya ibn Khalid ibn Barmak ('ibn' means 'son of'), his brother Muhammad and his two sons Al-Fadl and Ja'far exerted a dominant influence over the administration of the empire. The ancestry of this family fascinated Muslim historians, and so we know a lot about it. They were originally Buddhists from the city of Balkh, the great Buddhist centre to the north of Bamiyan across the mountains. 'Barmak', the name of Yahya's grandfather, was the Sanskrit word *pramukha*, 'leader': in other words, the grandfather of Yahya was the last of a line of hereditary abbots of the enormous Buddhist monastery at Balkh known as the Nawbahar. Their position had made the family spectacularly wealthy, with huge landownings around the city of Balkh. But these local magnates then successfully stepped up to the bigger stage of the Abbasid Empire and its magnificent capital at Baghdad, becoming powerful viziers and administrators to the early Abbasids, but also proverbial to this day in the Arab world for immense wealth and generous patronage, including in the arts and scholarship. The Barmakids experienced a sudden, mysterious fall from grace later in the reign of Harun al-Rashid, whose accession they had helped to engineer, but for whose tastes they may have been getting rather too powerful. But Ja'far, the vizier and close companion of Harun, lived on in stories that came to be incorporated into the *Thousand and One Nights*, where we also find the tale of the 'Barmecide Feast', in which a rich man tests a beggar's sense of humour by serving to him a series of imaginary courses. The tale plays off the Barmakids' wealth, sophistication, and ultimately also generosity. Ja'far the vizier has more recently gone to the bad, I have to report – the evil antagonist in the classic 1940 movie *The Thief of Bagdad* and the Disney animation *Aladdin* (1992).

The Barmakids become relevant to our story in their role as patrons of learning. It was through their good offices, and characteristic openmindedness, that much Greek science was incorporated into Islamic scholarship. But the Barmakids also exploited their ancestral position at the boundary of Islam and India (the Balkh–Bamiyan–Peshawar route being one of the gateways to India) to communicate Indian wisdom to the Islamic world. One consequence of this is that one of the most informative accounts of Buddhist Bamiyan was written by and for Muslims, and in the language of Islam, Arabic. This account is to be found in a remarkable text known as the *Fihrist* of Al-Nadim, a tenth-century catalogue of books

17. The evil Grand Vizier Jaffar (played by Conrad Veidt) in the classic movie *The Thief of Bagdad* (1940). The character of Jaffar is a development of Ja'far the vizier of Harun al-Rashid in the *Thousand and One Nights*, himself a memory of the great eighth-century Abbasid administrator Ja'far al-Barmaki, son of Yahya. Ja'far's great-grandfather had been abbot of the Buddhist monastery at Balkh.

which has been described as 'an encyclopedia or a compendium of the knowledge possessed by a learned Muslim in tenth-century Baghdad'. In a section of the *Fihrist* entitled 'The Names and Places of Worship in the Land of India, with a Description of the Buildings and the State of the Idols', we find a truly priceless description (or sequence of descriptions) of Bamiyan. The ultimate source of at least some of this information, we are told, is Yahya the grandson of Barmak, who at some point in the mid- to late-eighth century had commissioned a man to visit India 'so that he might bring him the medicinal plants found in that land and also write for him about the religions'. This chimes well with other interests of Yahya, who had Indian scholars of medicine and doctors brought to Baghdad, and Indian medicinal texts translated into Arabic. (Another name mentioned by Al-Nadim in connection with this account of Bamiyan is also suggestive: Al-Kindi, in whose handwriting Al-Nadim found the text he quotes for us, was a great Arab philosopher of the ninth century and a central figure in the transmission of Greek wisdom to the Islamic world.)

The passages from the *Fihrist* on Bamiyan clearly suffer from later editorial confusion, for example mixing up material on Bamiyan with a great Hindu temple of the sun-god Surya at Multan, in modern Pakistan. 'There is a building at al-Multan,' the account begins, but what follows seems rather to be describing Bamiyan:

> *In it there is an iron idol which is seven cubits in length. It is under the centre of a dome which magnetic stones support with balanced pressure on all sides. It is said that it leans to one side because of some injury. This temple is at the foot of a mountain.*

The height of its dome is one hundred and eighty cubits. The people of India [i.e. non-Muslims] make pilgrimages to it by land and sea from the farthest parts of their country. The road to it from Balkh is a straight one, for the regions of al-Multan are near to the districts of Balkh. On top of the mountain, as well as at its foot, there are houses for devotees and ascetics, as well as places for sacrificial victims and offerings. It is said that there is never a spare moment or a single hour when there are no people going there as pilgrims.

Here we may be getting a distorted account of the Great Stupa excavated by Professor Tarzi: we can certainly see the caves in the cliff face. The next part of the text is very clearly about Bamiyan, but doesn't betray any exceptional familiarity with the place:

They have two idols, one of which is called Jun-bukt and the other Zun-bukt. Their forms are carved out of the sides of a great valley, cut from the rock of the mountain. The height of each one of them is eighty cubits, so that they can be seen from a great distance.

But what follows is as valuable a testimony for Buddhist Bamiyan as Xuanzang's account, for it modulates in a fascinating way into the perceptions of a Buddhist worshipper:

The people of India go on pilgrimages to these two [idols], bearing with them offerings, incense and fragrant woods. If the eye should fall upon them from a distance, a man would be obliged to lower his eyes, overawed by them. If he is lacking in attention or careless when he sees them, it is necessary for him to return to a place from

which he cannot view them and then to approach them, seeking
them as an object for his attention with reverence for them.

We then abruptly return to an outsider's viewpoint, and get more of a sense of the barbarian and alien character of Buddhist Bamiyan, as seen from the perspective of an adherent of Islam. The report seems to confuse the dedication by monks of their lives to service in the monasteries with a literal sacrifice of life:

A man who has been an eyewitness of them told me that the
amount of blood which is shed beside them is not small in quan-
tity. He asserted that it might happen that perhaps about fifty
thousand or more might offer themselves, but it is Allah who
knows.

Finally, the text of the *Fihrist* turns explicitly to Bamiyan as if for the first time:

They have a building at Bamiyan on the frontiers of India,
where it borders on Sijistan. Ya'qub ibn Laith reached this local-
ity when he sought to invade India. The idols which were sent to
the City of Peace [i.e. Baghdad] from that locality of Bamiyan
were transported at the time of its invasion. Ascetics and devotees
occupy this great building. In it there are idols of gold adorned
with precious stones, the number of which is unknown and to
which no praise or description can do justice. The people of India
go there on pilgrimages by land and sea from the furthest town
of their country.

This last passage is the best evidence that Buddhism

was still being practised at Bamiyan when Ya'qub ibn Laith attacked in about 870, but we have seen already that the precise circumstances of Ya'qub's incursion are hazy. Some reference to the monastic buildings at Bamiyan is also discernible. But what this material clearly shows is how Bamiyan was presented to the Muslim intelligentsia of tenth-century Baghdad, and it was as a marvellous place, the site of remarkable buildings and artefacts even aside from the Buddhas, and the focus of worship from far and wide among non-Muslim peoples – an encapsulation of all that was strange and fascinating about the world beyond the boundaries of Islam. Quite how much of this material comes from Yahya's man is open to debate, but the role of the Barmakid clan as mediators between East and West is very clear, as is the continuing role of Bamiyan as boundary marker between the Islamic Occident and un-Islamic Orient. It will become clearer still in the next chapter how closely Bamiyan's celebrity is bound up with the waxing and waning of its strategic importance. In the sixth century, and again in the nineteenth century, Bamiyan occupied a position of great value to neighbouring powers. In the early Islamic centuries Bamiyan mattered just as much as a place where the limits of an Iranian and Indian sphere of secular and religious power were being contested and defined, and where those two spheres encountered each other, and necessarily also, whether they liked it or not, communicated with each other. Before we leave the Barmakids, it is worth acknowledging that some detailed early Islamic accounts of the great Buddhist monastery at Balkh, the Nawbahar, its physical character and its ritual life, underlay part of my reconstruction of Buddhist Bamiyan in the previous chapter. Those accounts are terribly confused about the religious affiliation of the Nawbahar, or the main stupa within it, for example claiming that it was a Zoroastrian shrine and modelled on the Ka'aba in Mecca (the focus of Muslim worship, believed to have been built by Abraham), but they can be traced back to another work indirectly indebted to the Barmakids, Al-Kirmani's work *Historical Accounts of the Barmakids and their Merits*.

The Barmakids, powerful in their day, and with a long lingering influence on Islamic administration and culture thereafter, give the lie to any attempt to draw sharp lines between Islam and what went before, or to define the Buddhas of Bamiyan as a monument somehow fundamentally incompatible with Islam. This Islamic encounter with India developed and deepened in following centuries, culminating in the Moghul Empire established by Babur in the sixteenth century. Between the Abbasids in Baghdad and the Moghuls in Delhi came one of the foremost intellectual figures of medieval Islam, Al-Biruni, astronomer, mathematician, natural scientist and much more (since he appeared to be interested in practically everything), who resided for at least the last three decades of his life at the splendid court of Mahmud of Ghazni and his successors, a centre for artistic and cultural achievements funded by Mahmud's military campaigns.

Al-Biruni's activities at Mahmud's court are particularly intriguing. Mahmud of Ghazni was the first great Islamic invader of India, notorious for his acts of iconoclasm there: he was the figure, we may recall, repeatedly cited by Mullah Omar as a model for the destruction of the Buddhas. Mahmud's most notorious act was the sacking of Somnath in Gujarat and the pillaging of the great temple of Shiva that stood there: the story goes that the cult image or *lingam* was broken up and pieces sent back to Ghazni for the faithful to walk upon. Every word of that is more myth than verifiable history, but Mahmud's sack of Somnath is also the context for the words imitated by Mullah Omar: offered money to spare the sacred image, Mahmud is meant to have insisted he was a breaker of idols, not a seller of them. Which makes Al-Biruni's enjoyment of Mahmud's patronage all the more interesting, since the flipside of Mahmud's undoubtedly violent encounter with India was the opportunity it offered Al-Biruni to compose his magnum opus, the *India* (more fully, *The Book Confirming What Pertains to India, Whether Rational or Despicable*), which he compiled from material gleaned either while accompanying Mahmud on campaign or, more likely, from captives brought back by Mahmud to Ghazni. It is a remarkably penetrating analysis of the Hindu world view, and launches some ideas that would be revisited by the British in the nineteenth century: for example, the notion that Indian thought and Greek thought (with which Al-Biruni was very familiar) came from the same ultimate source. This idea made sense to an Islamic intellectual trying to organise the knowledge inherited from non-Islamic cultures, but also appealed to British theorists seeking to justify European involvement in Indian affairs. For Al-Biruni Indian religion and learning was a new and intellectually stimulating set of materials to lay alongside the legacy of Greeks like Aristotle, and from this same fascination for the Indian cultures at the edge of the Islamic world came another of his works, the loss of which must be a source of great regret to us. What Al-Biruni wrote in his *Account of the Two Idols of Bamiyan* we cannot now say. But that this giant of medieval intellectual culture studied the Buddhas of Bamiyan in the court of Mahmud of Ghazni speaks volumes about the complexities of Islamic attitudes to idols.

One of the most interesting consequences of the weakening of the central rule of the caliphate in Baghdad, which encouraged the rise of more local powers such as Mahmud of Ghazni, is what is sometimes called the 'Persian renaissance', a reaction against Arabic influence in what is now eastern Iran and Afghanistan, which saw the reassertion of Persian as the language of culture and the rediscovery of pre-Islamic Persian culture and history. The great epic account of pre-Islamic Persian history, the *Shahnama* by the poet Ferdawsi, another resident at Mahmud's court, is the classic example of this Persian revival, still the 'national epic' of all Persian speakers. A more subtle indication of how pre-Islamic culture filtered back into Islamic culture of the eleventh century (and later) is the motif of the idol-like beloved found in Persian lyric poetry, imagery ultimately derived (it has been argued) from the Buddhism that preceded Islam in eastern Persia. Onsori was another poet at Mahmud's court in Ghazni, and the opening quatrain of one of his love lyrics conveys a huge amount about the influence of pagan idolatry on Islamic poetic forms, and indeed how complex and ambivalent an attitude to idolatry might be communicated there. Onsori praises his beloved with reference to idols, and to Azer, the maker of idols whose son was the great iconoclast Abraham:

> The idol which an idol-maker makes is not charming:
> Charm is not a capacity of the idol-maker.
> My idol steals my heart because their face is
> Like something Azer made but not the handiwork of Azer.

Onsori was also responsible for what may have been the oddest Islamic response to the Buddhas. His poem 'Khing but wa Surkh but', 'The Moon-white idol and the Red', is again unfortunately lost, but it was most likely a courtly romance, since we learn elsewhere that '*Khing but* is the loved one of *Surkh but*' and '*Surkh but* is the lover of *Khing but*'. 'Surkh but' and 'Khing but' became early on the established ways of identifying the larger and smaller Buddhas at Bamiyan, and we have already considered evidence that the colours of the Buddhas as they appeared to early Islamic witnesses reflected the statues' Buddhist-era colour scheme. The names clung to the images longer than any obvious decoration can have done. We first encounter them in an anonymous tenth-century Persian work of geography, the *Hodud al-Alam*, 'Regions of the World' (also the last place where the king of Bamiyan is called by his ancient Persian title of *shir*), and it is how they are still being named in compendia of the Moghul period: such as the *Farhang-i Jahangiri*, a seventeenth-century dictionary named in honour of Babur's great-grandson, the Moghul emperor Jahangir; and the *A'in-i Akbari*, 'Institutes of Akbar', a record of the administration of Akbar, Jahangir's father, the third volume of the much larger *Akbarnama*, the official chronicle of Akbar's reign. The related notion that the three Buddhas (larger, smaller, and the most complete of the seated Buddhas in-between) represent a man, woman and child is well established by this stage, and isn't fully extinguished among Western visitors until the twentieth century.

THE 'MULE MONASTERY'

Fundamentally, the Buddhas of Bamiyan found a place in the

new Muslim world because of the perfect way they responded to certain powerful themes in the literary and intellectual life of medieval Islam. There was a fascination for the extent of the Islamic world, reflected in concern for the variety of things to be found within it, and also its limits, geographical and otherwise. Not unrelatedly, medieval Islam saw a flourishing literature of Wonders, *'aja'ib* and *ghara'ib*, records of the remarkable and outlandish. In the eleventh century the writer Sam'ani, from whom Zemaryalai Tarzi indirectly drew his account of the Great Stupa of Bamiyan (which offered the Buddhas serious competition as a marvel in early Islamic accounts), records the view that the Buddhas 'have no equal in this world', while according to another seventeenth-century Moghul dictionary, the *Farhang-i Rashidi* (this time named after its compiler, Rashid, though it was dedicated to Shah Jahan, who built the Taj Mahal), the Khing But 'is one of the marvels (*'aja'ib*) of the age'. Similarly the Surkh But, 'in the same mountain, counts among astonishing works (*ghara'ib*)'.

But when Islamic texts express wonder at the Buddhas, it is never quite wonder for its own sake, but rather wonder at the infinitely creative power of God. A representative account of Bamiyan, which will also take us back to our earlier thoughts on Islamic unease about idols, is the *'Aja'ib al-makhluqat*, 'Wonders of Creation', by Tusi, dedicated to the last sultan of the Great Seljuq Empire in the later twelfth century. In part of it Tusi considers 'The wonders of carved and painted images' and 'Strange images', and in that second category he includes the Buddhas of Bamiyan, treading a fine line between an acknowledgement that image-making is *haram*, 'unlawful', and an insistence that these man-made wonders can nevertheless embody God's benign influence in the world. Tusi prefaces the section in which he mentions Bamiyan with a carefully formulated reflection on the nature of these 'talismanic' images:

> *We will relate another section on other images which are talismanic so that you will know that the Creator gives divine inspiration to His subjects to make such wonders. And you know that that is from His power, not from the power of the created one, just as you do not consider writing as from the pen but from the hand of the writer.*

Tusi's view of these wonders, in other words, is that they reveal the hand of the Islamic Creator, working through humans: the wonders are in actual fact evidence of Allah's providential care for humankind. In his account of the Buddhas of Bamiyan, at any rate, there is no sense that the Buddhas are incompatible with Islam, but rather that in some ineffable way they are attuned to God's design in the world:

> *In the region of Bamiyan there is a place called 'Astar Bahar'. They have made two images, each one 250 cubits tall with crowns on their heads. They call one 'Moon-white Idol' and the other 'Red Idol'. Pigeons nest in their noses. When the sun rises they both smile. This I have seen in many books, but the meaning of their smile is not known – God knows best. This smile should not be thought strange, for whatever the sun shines on, cheerfulness and joviality appear in it, and that thing inclines towards the sun.*

The name Tusi uses for Bamiyan, Astar Bahar, carries a reminiscence of a Buddhist monastery, a *vihara* in Sanskrit, as at the Nawbahar (*nava vihara*, 'New Monastery') in Balkh. ('Astar' means 'mule'!) The religious charge that the Buddhas continued to carry in the Islamic era is remarkable (wrongly estimated at 250 cubits, about 115m, they would indeed have been incredibly high), but even such ambivalence as Tusi does allow himself to express about images is nothing entirely new in the religious history of Bamiyan. One might see Tusi's Buddhas continuing to share in that dialectic between the visible and the inexpressible so essential to Buddhist iconography, conveying despite themselves, in both cases, the humbling wonder of God's creation.

What we are perhaps lacking in this collection of reactions to the Buddhas is an eyewitness. Most of the accounts of Bamiyan in Islamic literature, Tusi's being a case in point, are at some remove from any immediate experience of the place: Bamiyan is something in books, and that distance can of course serve to amplify its mystery and wonder. But a final example will bring us back to the sixteenth century, within a few years of Babur's tribulations in the wintry Hindu Kush, and as close to the statues as it is possible to get. Sultan Muhammad, a *mufti* or scholar from Balkh, also experienced severe weather conditions as he crossed the Hindu Kush. His book *Majma' al-ghara'ib*, 'Miscellany of Extraordinary Things', is a collection of wonders of Creation presented to a new ruler of Balkh. Among the marvels is Bamiyan, of which the author is able to give an unmediated account, since, as he says, 'The writer of these words, when he was headed for Kabul from the city of Balkh, came to this place on Tuesday the 14th of Rabi' al-Thani in the year 935 [26 December 1528].' The caravan with which Sultan Muhammad was travelling was caught up in a violent storm as it passed through

18. Wilfred Thesiger's photograph of a trader at the head of a line of camels, carrying bags of lucerne (a fodder crop) from Besud in the Hazarajat to Jalalabad. The image, from 1954, captures an activity essentially unchanged for centuries. Camel caravans like this one were the lifeblood of Bamiyan throughout its history, plying the route from Jalalabad and Kabul to Balkh or Mazar-i Sharif, and resting and securing supplies at Bamiyan mid-way.

Bamiyan, and everybody took shelter in the Buddha niches, 'a hundred men with the camels and mules' in the larger niche, while 'another group of about three hundred men and horses and mules found respite in the other niche of the female idol' (recall that the two Buddhas were generally interpreted as man and wife). The use of the Buddha niches and neighbouring caves by passing caravans is also recorded in nineteenth-century accounts, but is perhaps something we can imagine happening ever since Buddhist times at the Mule Monastery. Muhammad describes the statues in detail, concluding with the comment, 'In the book *Jahannama* ['Book of the World'] it is said that these two idols are Yaghuth and Ya'uq, but it is Almighty God who knows the truth.' Yaghuth and Ya'uq are characters from the Qur'an, false gods: Noah's warnings fall on deaf ears, and the people soon to be drowned in the Flood for their rejection of the true God say to one another, 'Abandon not your gods: Abandon neither Wadd nor Suwa', neither Yaguth nor Ya'uq, nor Nasr.' Another source on Bamiyan tells us that one of the seated Buddhas was identified with Nasr. Sultan Muhammad suspects, therefore, that the Buddhas represent two quite archetypal enemies of the faith, and the Islamic credentials of this *mufti* are unimpeachable, but he shows no inclination to damage them, or indeed to regard them as anything but heaven-sent blessings – and Extraordinary Things, of course.

Sultan Muhammad's appealing little anecdote thus represents a more authentically Islamic response to the Buddhas than, for example, Goethe's. In the notes accompanying a section of Goethe's homage to the Persian poet Hafez, *West-östlicher Divan* (1819), he delivers a panegyric of Zoroastrianism, 'a pure religion of nature', and comments on its commendable resistance to the influence of 'Indian idol worship'. Goethe sets Bamiyan, with its 'crazy idols established and worshipped on a gigantic scale', in contrast with Balkh, where the civilising force of Zoroastrianism, according to Goethe, held sway. One indication of Zoroastrian Balkh's grandeur, and the superiority of the Zoroastrian religion, he continues, was the great men it had produced – the family of the Barmakids. Unfortunately, Goethe was led astray by Islamic sources which had mistaken the origins of the Barmakids, thinking their ancestors were Zoroastrian priests. In actual fact that remarkable family, descendants of the abbots of the great Buddhist monastery in Balkh, was just as much a product of 'Indian idol worship' as the Buddhas of Bamiyan. In general Goethe's collection achieves a remarkable synthesis of his own Enlightenment world and the Islamic and pre-Islamic cultures of Persia, but it is achieved at the cost of absolute rejection of another face of Asian spirituality, the (in Goethe's view) inferior religious culture of polytheism, which he considered exemplified by the Buddhas of Bamiyan. As he inveighs against idols, the presiding genius of German literature has been described as looking like 'a Christian missionary, a Muslim iconoclast or even a Taliban ideologue'. To that I would only add that, as we now appreciate if we didn't before, Goethe is stereotyping what was in actual fact a complex and diverse set of attitudes held by Muslims throughout history to figurative representations in general, and the Buddhas of Bamiyan in particular. To employ a turn of phrase that is surprisingly common in contemporary Iran, Goethe is being *katoliktar az Pap*, 'More Catholic than the Pope', since iconoclasm plays a much larger part in caricatures of Islam than it ever has in the real thing.

Earlier we traced historical developments in Bamiyan as far as 1221, and we discovered that the history of medieval Afghanistan was as intricate as any other period in this geologically and culturally marginal space. That history could also be very, very bloody. The Ghurid rulers of the twelfth century, who established an empire based at Firuzkuh in the mountains east of Bamiyan, and used Bamiyan as a kind of subsidiary capital, set the bar quite high in this regard. The Ghurid king who was first to bring Bamiyan under Ghurid control and who burned the city of Ghazni in 1150/1 earned the Persian soubriquet 'Jahansuz', 'World-burner', for his brutality. A later Ghurid ruler of Bamiyan killed an uncle who had seized power in his absence, and had a disloyal vizier flayed alive. But the devastation that came to Afghanistan and to Bamiyan with the Mongols in 1221 was of a quite different order. The anthropologist Thomas Barfield tells an anecdote that speaks eloquently of the profound effects of the Mongol invasion, a disaster from which Afghanistan has arguably never fully recovered. An illiterate man in northern Afghanistan was describing to Barfield a great irrigation system with six major canals, only three of which were still operating. Afghanistan was a much better place when all the canals were working, he told Barfield: 'you should have visited us then'. The damage that the man was describing had actually been done by Genghis Khan in the thirteenth century, but for that Afghan it was still tangible. The destruction of cities and the irrigation works on which agriculture depended, and the colossal loss of life, eclipsed everything that had gone before. A century later the great traveller Ibn Battuta visited Balkh, a city whose power and importance we have repeatedly stressed, and described a ghost town: 'It is completely dilapidated and uninhabited, but anyone seeing it would think it to be inhabited because of the solidity of its construction (for it was a vast and important city), and its mosques and colleges preserve their outward appearance even now, with the inscriptions on their buildings incised with lapis-blue paints.' In 1222 a Chinese monk, Chang Chun, summoned to meet Genghis in Afghanistan, had passed Balkh very soon after its sack on his way home, empty apart from the dogs whose barking he could hear.

Genghis's assault on northern Afghanistan is best understood as a mopping-up operation after his defeat of the Khwarazmian Empire, but seeking a motivation is probably beside the point. When the Mongol forces came to Bamiyan, the story goes, Genghis's brutality was sharpened by the death of his favourite grandson. The account is given by the Persian historian Juvaini, writing a generation later:

> *Starting from there the Mongols came to Bamiyan, the inhabitants of which place issued forth in hostility and resistance, and on both sides hands were laid to arrows and catapults. Suddenly, by the thumb of Fate, who was the destroyer of all that people, a bolt, which gave no respite, was discharged from the town and hit a son of Chagatai, the favourite grandchild of Genghis Khan. The Mongols made the greater haste to capture the town, and when it was taken Genghis gave orders that every living creature, from mankind down to the brute beasts, should be killed; that no prisoner should be taken; that not even the child in its mother's womb should be spared; and that henceforth no living creature should dwell therein. He gave it the name Ma'u-Baligh, which in Persian is 'Bad Town'. And to this day no living creature has taken up abode there.*

For all Juvaini's rhetorical embellishment, it is a chilling story. The level of destruction, at least, seems real enough. According to Ibn Battuta, 'Genghis massacred the inhabitants of Bamiyan, and destroyed it from top to bottom, with the exception of the minaret of its Friday Mosque' – it must have been a haunting sight, that isolated minaret. Ibn Battuta himself, making for India, crossed from Balkh to Kabul by a pass further to the east, no doubt partly because Bamiyan can have had little to offer passing travellers in his day. The events of 1221 amounted, in the words of one scholar, to 'the reduction of the old and illustrious city to an insignificant village'. When human occupation resumed, Bamiyan was an agricultural space, and only fairly recently has a small town been re-established.

Of course, the Buddhas survived, any damage allegedly done to them by Genghis strictly in the realms of myth, and in time also the valley of Bamiyan was repopulated by the people who now predominate in Bamiyan, the ethnic group known as the Hazaras. What seems to have happened, piecing the story together from folk traditions and occasional pointers in the historical record, is that control of most of modern Afghanistan by the successors of Chagatai, son of Genghis (and father of the man whose death allegedly provoked the destruction of Bamiyan in 1221), led to the settlement of Mongol troops and their families in the characteristically Mongol military-cum-social unit of the *minghan* (in Persian *hazara*, 'a thousand', hence 'Hazara'), in the context, unsurprisingly, of designs upon India, which made places like Bamiyan once again strategically critical.

Some such reconstruction at any rate makes sense of persistent folk beliefs about the origins of the Hazaras which have recently received quite dramatic support from the developing science of human evolutionary genetics. One of the benefits of our ever-increasing understanding of the human genome is a set of astonishingly informative tools for reconstructing human history through the identification of genetic patterns and divergences. Put simply, human DNA is prone, very occasionally, to mutation, and once a mutation has occurred, it is passed on to descendants, an inbuilt lineage carried around by all of us, if only it can be deciphered. A comparatively straightforward kind of genetic history is provided by the Y chromosome, passed from father to son, and it was research on the Y chromosome that in 2003 turned abstruse science into column inches under headlines like 'We owe it all to superstud Genghis' and 'Genghis super-Y: the gene for a true alpha male'. Each man's Y chromosome should differ very slightly, but what the researchers uncovered was a huge number of all-but identical Y chromosomes spread over an extremely wide area of central and east Asia. A common ancestor for this genetic 'haplotype' could be traced to Mongolia, roughly 1,000 years ago. The speed and breadth of its diffusion made it certain that the agency for its stunning success lay with Genghis Khan and his male relatives. And while the prevalence of the haplotype in general mapped rather neatly onto the territory conquered by Genghis and ruled by his successors, an interesting exception were Hazaras tested in Pakistan, a population resulting from emigrations in the wake of rebellion and persecution in late-nineteenth-century Afghanistan, in whom an exceptionally high manifestation of the 'Genghis haplotype' was identified.

Particular gene types gain prominence by two recognised processes: the familiar Darwinian principle of natural

19. A Hazara man from Deh Zangi, south of Bamiyan, 1954 photographed by Wilfred Thesiger. The Hazaras are the dominant ethnic group in Bamiyan, and fascinating light on their origins has been shed by recent genetic research.

selection, which ensures the success over time of any type with a competitive advantage, and what geneticists call 'genetic drift' (an extreme version of which is called 'founders' effect'), the fillip randomly given any particular haplotype if it happens to be possessed by a genetically influential individual or individuals. An interestingly controversial case, which potentially illustrates the working of both these principles, is the near universal prevalence of the type O blood group among Native Americans, even though they seem to be descended from an Asian population with a group O frequency of around 50 per cent. One explanation credits the phenomenon to natural selection: type O seems to convey some degree of resistance to syphilis, a disease prevalent in the Americas before European contact (whether or not that contact introduced it to Europe is a much-debated question). But another possible explanation is that the first, potentially very small group of colonists of the Americas, the pioneering Asian 'founders' of the Native American population who crossed the land bridge now covered by the Bering Straits, just happened to be group O, and bequeathed that blood type to their descendants. If natural selection is 'survival of the fittest', genetic drift has been called a case of 'survival of the luckiest'. Genghis Khan's genetic signature is a spectacular example of the 'founders' effect', and the prominence of the type among Pakistani Hazaras, always assuming that group is representative of the larger population in Afghanistan, confirms the likelihood of an essentially Mongol origin. Study of the dialect of Persian spoken by the Hazaras has led to similar conclusions: it contains a significant proportion of Mongol elements, presumably the vestiges of a language once spoken in the area. (Babur seems to indicate that Mongol was spoken in some parts of the mountains in the early sixteenth century.) This is a mixed blessing since, while a source of pride to some Hazaras, the belief in their descent from Genghis and his armies has stoked prejudice against the Hazaras in a country where, as Thomas Barfield discovered in his chat about irrigation systems, the past resists being safely consigned to history.

HAZRAT-I ALI

Much changed with the Mongol invasion, but certain things remained: the stunning natural beauty of Bamiyan, for example, and the colossal stone Buddhas. In time, too, the new inhabitants of Bamiyan were Islamised, although for reasons that are unclear the Hazaras are overwhelmingly Shiʻa, another cause of tension with the Sunni majority of Afghanistan. Over time, too, the local population have developed their own folklore to explain the remarkable place they inhabit. One of the very earliest European visitors, Edward Stirling, arrived in Bamiyan, as it happens, three hundred years to the day after Sultan Muhammad (on 26 December 1828), and in similarly inclement weather. He was not particularly impressed by the Buddhas, and the modern editor of his journals, Jonathan Lee (himself a leading light in contemporary Afghan studies), has wondered whether Stirling's disappointment with the place was because of the time of year he arrived, when 'the valley was devoid of the grass, fruit and poplar trees which, during the spring and summer, make the valley one of the most spectacular sights of Afghanistan'. But Stirling did like the story he heard told about the statues: 'They have nothing to recommend them except their singular appearance in the wall, and the tradition the natives tell of them in praise of their present religion and the efforts of *Shah Mardan* and Murtaz Ally Sheer.' It is not clear whether Stirling realises that the 'Shah Mardan' and 'Murtaz Ally Sheer' who featured in the folk tales he heard are in fact one and the same person, all names of Ali, the cousin and son-in law of the Prophet, who is important to all Muslims but especially (as the first Imam, and Muhammad's proper successor, and indeed a figure second in importance only to the Prophet) among the Shi'a. What Stirling heard was one of many legends of Hazrat-i Ali: we have seen already how a strange volcanic formation to the west of Bamiyan, the Azhdaha ('Dragon'), became the focus of storytelling about him. Similar tales of the hero, riding his horse Duldul and wielding the sword Zulfiqar, explain other features of the landscape: the remarkable series of lakes at Band-i Amir, separated by dams formed by mineral deposits, have an especially rich cycle of stories associated with them, hinted at in their evocative names: 'Dam of Zulfiqar', 'Dam of Mint', 'Dam of Cheese', 'Dam of Awe', 'The Groom's Dam' and 'The Slaves' Dam'. 'Band-i Amir' means 'Dam of the Commander', and refers to Ali himself. The gist of the legend is the defeat of an oppressive king, and the conversion of the king and his people to Islam.

The people of Bamiyan thus became Islamic, but so also, through their storytelling, became the physical environment, and the local people's accounts of the Buddhas, among all those we have seen and shall see in this book, deserve a special prominence. A lovely book was published in 1953 by the Musée Guimet in Paris, where a lot of material from Bamiyan is held. *Légendes et coutumes afghanes* is attributed to Marie Hackin (known universally as 'Ria') and Ahmad Ali Kohzad, but in truth Hackin and her husband Joseph, director of the French archaeological mission in Afghanistan (DAFA), had been killed in 1941 when their ship was torpedoed. *Légendes* is Kohzad's tribute to Ria Hackin: 'It seems I see her still seated beside me, opposite the old blind storyteller of Bamiyan.' On the Buddhas, Hackin and Kohzad talk of the numerous legends attached to them, for example the marvellous story that survivors of Noah's Ark modelled the figures in the earth still a little wet and malleable after the Flood, in homage to God. But the commoner story was the one told to Stirling, which made the larger Buddha the warrior Salsal and the smaller his wife Shahmama:

Salsal, known for his acts of gallantry, was the most famous warrior in the whole region of Bamiyan. Thanks to his extraordinary fighting spirit, he had succeeded in imposing his law on the peoples of Bamiyan who, while dreading him, admired him greatly. At the time of the Muslim conquest, he defended the country admirably against the new invader; he went as far as to take the fight to the enemy, who fled, terrified.

The defenders of Islam, mercilessly repulsed, no longer dared to return to the attack and decided by common accord to go and ask the advice of the Prophet in order to request his help and protection. To achieve an audience more quickly, they had brought an arrow which had belonged to this famous barbarian, an arrow so heavy that six ordinary beings gave way beneath its weight.

To resolve this new problem, the Prophet appealed to the clear-sightedness of his son-in-law, the famous Ali, who was given the mission to fight this infidel. He set out immediately. The moment he was on the field of combat, he was obliged to conclude very quickly that it would be impossible for him to defeat this adversary, since the man was clad in a coat of mail belonging to Hazrat-i Daoud [the prophet David]: it possessed the special quality of containing in each of its links pious words from the holy book.

In a terrible quandary, Ali found himself quite unable to join battle. So he considered returning to Medina to ask the advice of the Prophet. However, the following night, he had a dream thanks to which he succeeded in bringing down his enemy. A spirit appeared to him and ordered him to carve an arrow in tamarisk wood; this arrow he should shoot into his adversary's eye.

Ali followed these instructions without delay. Salsal received in his right eye an injury so painful that he had to flee away, moaning. He sought refuge in a well. Having seen his flight, his supporters gave up the struggle and submitted to the invader.

Hazrat-i Ali, tender and generous heart, had pity for his adversary. Approaching the well, he cried: 'If you accept the word of God, I shall give you back your eye.' In the end Salsal accepted Ali's conditions. Taken out of the pit, the recovery occurred immediately, thanks to the miraculous touch of fingers wetted with the saliva of Hazrat-i Ali.

4

....

ON THE TRAIL OF ALEXANDER

One sword-knot stolen from the camp
Will pay for all the school expenses
Of any Kurrum Valley scamp
Who knows no word of moods and tenses,
But, being blessed with perfect sight,
Picks off our messmates left and right.

Rudyard Kipling, from 'Arithmetic on the Frontier'

IF THERE IS A PARADISE ON EARTH ...

There is an eye-catching nineteenth-century image of Shahr-i Zohak, the castle perched on red cliffs at the eastern end of the Bamiyan valley. It is a lithograph after a drawing of 1840 by Lieutenant John Sturt of the Bengal Engineers, and it is a charming scene. In the foreground is one of the channels of the Bamiyan river after its merger with another river from the south, and beside it, in the morning sunshine, a group of men have eaten breakfast and are loading the camels in preparation for departure. Behind them is lush vegetation and farmland, dotted with cattle and sheep, and forming the impressive backdrop to the whole scene, the towering cliffs of Zohak, fortifications balanced precariously on its steep sides

20. A lithograph of Shahr-i Zohak, based on a drawing made by Lieut. John Sturt, Bengal Engineers, on the morning of 23 August, 1840. The castle guards the entrance to the Bamiyan valley, to the right of the image, and controls the routes from north, east and south that meet beneath it. Sturt and his companion Rollo Burslem were on an expedition to survey the passes over the Hindu Kush during the British occupation of Afghanistan in the First Anglo-Afghan War.

and summits. The scene is exaggerated, the cliffs higher than they are in reality, the valley more idyllically pastoral. But I can say from personal experience of one of the most beautiful places I have seen that Sturt didn't exaggerate so much. The vegetation below Shahr-i Zohak is an intense green against the red cliffs rising starkly from the valley floor, punctuated by the elaborate brickwork of man-made towers. Everything is accompanied by the bubbling of the water in the intricate irrigation system supplying the fields from the river channels that criss-cross the valley floor.

In Sturt's image, and in my experience, it is an intensely peaceful scene. But for me, and surely for Lieutenant Sturt also, the impression of tranquillity was the more compelling for the hints of violence all around. I was reading Rodric Braithwaite's *Afgantsy*, on the Soviet occupation of Afghanistan, and struggled to divorce my response to this scene from what he says about the Russian experience of fighting in irrigated fields and narrow valleys: this lovely environment easily becomes a killing zone. Shahr-i Zohak was probably abandoned in the thirteenth century, after the attack of Genghis Khan, but it has been a military installation more recently than that. Mines and unexploded ordnance from the Soviet occupation and the civil war used to litter the site, and here and elsewhere along the narrow valleys of the Hindu Kush, the minefields (being patiently cleared one at a time by demining teams) keep pace with ancient fortifications, strongpoints in the Middle Ages still being strongpoints in the 1990s. In the very highest turret of Shahr-i Zohak there are the remains of a modern anti-aircraft gun.

We can date Sturt's sketch with precision, because his companion Captain Rollo Burslem later wrote a book, disarmingly titled *A Peep into Toorkisthan*, describing their activities in the Hindu Kush. It was the summer of 1840, and the British had recently invaded Afghanistan to restore to the throne the pretender Shah Shuja al-Mulkh (who had been deposed in 1809), imagining that they would thereby create a friendly buffer state beyond the north-west border of British India. Lieutenant Sturt had been instructed to survey the all-important passes at the northern edge of Shah Shuja's territory. (At this juncture Afghanistan, more accurately known as the Kingdom of Kabul, stopped at the Hindu Kush: it now extends north as far as the River Oxus or Amu Darya.) On their route back the two officers visited Zohak, or at least Captain Burslem did: Sturt was recovering from an attack of 'Koondooz fever' (malaria) and probably stayed in camp rather than making the physically demanding ascent. Sturt's sketch must date to the next morning, 23 August 1840, as the party prepared to set off back towards Kabul.

It is no surprise that the seductive image of the 'Ruins of Zohauk' was really the product of a military expedition. In a little over a year Sturt would be dead, mortally wounded during the chaotic and bloody retreat of a British column through the passes from Kabul to Jalalabad during the First Anglo-Afghan War of 1839–42, one of the most notorious and mythologised events in Britain's imperial history. By a twist of fate, Sturt's widow Alexandrina, his mother-in-law Florentia, Lady Sale, and his baby daughter Julia Florentia, would visit Bamiyan themselves in the wake of that catastrophe, taken prisoner during the massacre in the passes. Lady Sale's bestselling journal of a hostage crisis which gripped the British nation would contribute significantly to the growing celebrity of the Buddhas of Bamiyan.

But the deeper reason for the Buddhas' return to fame in the mid-nineteenth century was, as always, their location. The most important route through the Hindu Kush, was, for the first time in many centuries, once again of international importance. Two empires, the British and the Russian, were converging on Afghanistan and to many the solid mountain boundary of the Hindu Kush – high, inhospitable and ninety miles thick – looked like the ideal boundary between them. In 1840, as Sturt sketched that early-morning scene, this secure frontier might appear to have been achieved. 'By the dispatch of a small contingent to Bamiyan to watch the passes over the main ridge,' Fraser-Tytler remarks, 'for the first and last time in history the British were in actual physical occupation of the great north-western frontier of their dominions.' In fact, the British would not stay in Afghanistan for long. But it was in the context of this British push to the north-west of India in pursuit of a satisfactory border that the Buddhas of Bamiyan achieved a place in the Western imagination which they have never entirely relinquished.

By 1846, when he published his memoir, Burslem had no need to 'detain the reader by any description either of the wonderful ruins of the ancient city of Goolgoolla or of the gigantic images of Bameeān', since quite a number of earlier visitors had done so. But as recently as the turn of the nineteenth century they had been effectively unknown in the West. Their champion, Captain Francis Wilford, was in many ways an unlikely one, eccentric and far too open-minded for his own good. In one respect, though, he was an authentic creature of the culture that rediscovered the Buddhas of Bamiyan: a growing empire obsessed with understanding and controlling territory. Like Sturt, Wilford was an officer of the Bengal

Engineers and a surveyor, based in Benares (Varanasi), but for our purposes also the author of a series of wildly speculative, but surprisingly influential (Shelley was a particular fan) contributions to the journal of the Asiatick Society of Bengal in Calcutta, *Asiatick Researches*. His most influential article of all was 'On Mount Caucasus', which filled eighty densely argued pages of Volume VI, published in Calcutta in 1799 and then in London in 1801. Its ultimate claim was nothing less than that in the Indian Caucasus – the Hindu Kush – was to be located the origins of the human race, and Bamiyan, a place at the time still far away from British territory and concomitantly exotic, was central to his argument. Wilford's introduction of Bamiyan to his argument is worthy of the impact it would have on the Western imagination: 'This famous city, the Thebes of the East [Wilford is thinking, like William Simpson a century later, of the Colossi of Memnon at Luxor in Egypt], being hardly known in Europe, I beg leave to lay before the Society a short description of it, with an abstract of its history.' The promised description is, in the circumstances, an impressively accurate account of the physical site of Bamiyan. (Perhaps we should expect no less of a military surveyor.) But the 'history' that follows is another matter entirely.

From the accounts of informants who had visited Bamiyan, the notice in the Moghul-era *A'in-i Akbari*, and a description of Bamiyan by the Oxford orientalist Thomas Hyde in his *Historia religionis veterum Persarum eorumque magorum* of 1700, itself indebted to Arabic and Persian sources, Wilford pieces together his description. He describes the route from Kabul to the Shibar Pass, then Zohak and Bamiyan; the 'small conical hill' of Gholghola, covered with ruins; 'a vast number of apartments, or recesses, cut out of the rock', some of them decorated although the paintings are generally coated with smoke; and the three statues in their niches at Bamiyan (the third perhaps the standing statue at Kakrak, rather than the seated Buddha west of the 38m figure), though Wilford doubts the fairly accurate measurements given in the *A'in-i Akbari*, and (completely unaware that they represent the Buddha) adopts the view which had been established at least since the time of the great Moghul-era dictionaries that the two statues represented a man and a woman (sometimes, as noted, specifically the pagan warrior Salsal and his wife Shahmama). He even has details of their decoration, the traces of red and grey colouring, and the damage they show, which allows Wilford a moment of cultural stereotyping: 'One of the legs of the male figure is much broken: for the *Musulmans* never march that way with cannon without firing two or three shots at them: but from their want of skill, they seldom do much mischief.'

The one respect in which Wilford's geographical information leads him seriously astray is his account of the rivers of the area. 'A rivulet,' he writes of the Bamiyan river, 'rising in the adjacent hills, goes through the ruins of *Ghulghuleh* and the *Tagavi* [district] of *Bamiyan*, and falls into a small lake, from which issue four rivers, the *Hirmend*, the *Landhi–Sindh*, the rivers of *Bahlac*, and of *Conduz*.' This single lake giving rise to all four rivers is a fantasy, a distortion of the geographical peculiarity noted by Babur: Bamiyan does indeed sit close to the watershed between the systems of the Oxus and Indus, and it is true that the Helmand, Qunduz (actually the continuation of the Bamiyan), Balkh and Ghurband rivers (the waters of the last of which eventually drain into the Indus) all rise not very far away – but not in exactly the same place!

However, it is this fiction of a single source that sparks Wilford's extraordinary claim about Bamiyan's place in human history.

But before we get to it, we should do Francis Wilford the kindness of setting him in context. Wilford's historical methodology will seem deeply peculiar to us, but it was not so untypical of the Asiatick Society of Bengal. The Asiatick Society, an attempt to set the British presence in Calcutta on a more intellectual basis, was established by the scholar and Sanskritist Sir William Jones in 1784. Jones's own broad interests in Indian language, literature and culture exerted great influence over the other members of the Society, but nothing did so more than his greatest insight: that Sanskrit bore a close enough relationship to Latin and Ancient Greek that the languages must share a common origin. Jones's Third Anniversary Discourse to the Society, delivered in February 1786 and published in volume I of *Asiatick Researches* two years later, marked an intellectual epoch, inaugurating the discipline of historical linguistics. But to Wilford and others the discovery of the Indo-European family of languages opened up the possibility of a fundamental unity of cultures. Jones himself in the Third Discourse goes on to claim, in echo of Al-Biruni, that in India 'we now live among the adorers of those very Deities who were worshipped under different names in old *Greece* and *Italy*; and among the professors of those philosophical tenets, which the *Ionick* and *Attick* writers illustrated with all the beauties of their melodious language' – in other words, parallels as strong as the linguistic could be assumed to exist between Indian and classical religion and philosophy. When Reuben Burrow, another surveyor and contributor to *Asiatick Researches*, drew the rather memorable conclusion that 'Stonehenge is evidently one of the temples of *Boodh*', he isn't actually moving far beyond claims about the diffusion of Hinduism made by Jones himself.

The members of the Asiatick Society can hardly be blamed for getting carried away by Jones's intoxicating idea. In Wilford's case it was partly because his Indian sources were often suspect (some of them, it later transpired, forged, without Wilford's knowledge, so as to provide him with the parallels he sought), but more because other disciplines had yet to catch up with Jones's insight. Reading Wilford reminds one how much was achieved in the nineteenth century in the intellectual sphere: it is a quite fundamental assumption of Wilford, for example, that the Bible offers indisputable information about the early history of the world, and in general his scholarship fits some cutting-edge modern tools into an essentially pre-modern intellectual framework. When, in the course of 'On Mount Caucasus', Wilford embarks on an investigation of Indian, Persian and biblical accounts of 'the progenitors of mankind', he is very soon in an intellectual project which would not have seemed out of place four centuries earlier. Making rather too liberal a use of the word 'obviously', and basing his case mainly on dubious etymology, Wilford identifies the place of origin of the very first humans as '*Bamiyan* and the adjacent countries'. Wilford's conclusion, delivered with more sangfroid than is strictly appropriate, is that 'we may then reasonably look for the terrestrial paradise in that country'. The clinching argument that Bamiyan was in actual fact the Garden of Eden is, of course, those four rivers running from it, for just as 'a river went out of Eden to water the garden; and from thence it was parted, and became into four heads', so 'a small brook winds through the *Tagavis* of *Bamiyan*, and falling into a small lake, divides itself into four heads, forming so many navigable rivers'. Geographically this is arrant nonsense, needless to say. But I confess I find it pleasing that the source of the idea of this lake is probably the tangle of river channels below Zohak, which is, for what it's worth, as good a candidate for the terrestrial paradise as I have experienced.

'SOMETHING WILD, STRANGE, AND NEW'

In the course of the nineteenth and twentieth centuries Afghanistan came to exert a powerful mystique for Westerners, and that was as true for East India Company officers in the early 1800s as it became for hippies 150 years later. The source of the appeal is hard to pin down, though we'll consider one important contributing factor, the Afghan campaigns of Alexander the Great, later in this chapter. It would certainly be rash to attribute too much to Wilford's article in *Asiatick Researches*, although it had a remarkably wide readership. But Wilford offered his readers an alluring terra incognita, albeit one which (in the way of colonial projections) turned out ultimately to be an unexpectedly familiar kind of place, if one followed Wilford's logic. What we can certainly say is that this is the period when that Western fascination for Afghanistan, which persists to this day, first began – and from that beginning Bamiyan always represented the quintessence of the Afghan experience. Not so long after Wilford's contribution, in 1808, when British fears were focused on Napoleonic France, Mountstuart Elphinstone found himself on the banks of the Indus, gazing across to the mountains of Afghanistan, and allowed his imagination to wander: 'On the other side of the range were tribes and places, of which we had never heard the names; while those we had learned from our maps, were equally new to our informants. All we could learn was, that beyond the hills was something wild, strange, and new, which we might hope one day to explore.' From Peshawar, the winter capital of the Amir of Afghanistan, which was as close as he got, Elphinstone still managed to write the most perceptive nineteenth-century account of Afghanistan, *An Account of the Kingdom of Caubul* (1815). One of the tantalisingly out-of-reach places beyond the mountains was Bamiyan, which he turns to at the end of his account of the Hazaras: 'I must not quit the Hazaurehs without noticing the celebrated idols of Baumeeaun, which stand within their country.'

When Wilford was writing 'On Mount Caucasus', Bamiyan was still a thousand miles from the edge of British-held territory. Afghanistan was far out of sight, though evidently not entirely out of mind. How far strategic thinking of the time influenced Wilford's speculations, it is hard to say. But it wasn't long before Afghanistan was at the very centre of British policy, and a generation of spies, scholars, soldiers and hostages would be able to verify Wilford's descriptions of Bamiyan at first hand. None of them, regrettably, would find any evidence of Eden, but their very presence there indicated a geographical centrality of another, less spiritual kind, the critical strategic importance which came to be attached by the British (and to some degree the Russians) to the passes through the Hindu Kush. And that perhaps is the greatest achievement of the wild flights of 'On Mount Caucasus': Bamiyan was back on the map.

Afghanistan's – and Bamiyan's – return to centrality in the nineteenth century was very much a European phenomenon, and predominantly a British one. What directed British minds, and eventually feet, towards the Hindu Kush was anxiety about the defensibility of the territory held by the East India Company, an irrational anxiety, but no less powerful a motivation for that. It was a complex anxiety, too. Although it might be presented (and indeed felt) as a fear of physical attack by external forces from the north-west, the more immediate concern was the potential for unrest *within* British territory. Malcolm Yapp, author of the seminal modern account of this period, talks of the 'conviction' of the British in India that they 'were sitting on a parcel of deliquescent gelignite', a subject people always on the point of revolting and rendering the British involvement in India, essentially a commercial operation, unprofitable and untenable. British expansion was thus primarily driven by the desire to deny first the French, and then the Russians the scope to foment seditious activities against British rule within India. What kept the pot bubbling was an exactly parallel set of anxieties on the Russian side. Once again there was fear from the more paranoid in Russian policy-making circles of a physical British invasion of central Asia, a space notoriously short of natural boundaries; but even calmer heads were unanimous in suspecting a British desire to exert a malign *influence* on peoples in Russia's backyard. Count Nesselrode, the Russian foreign minister, complained to the Russian ambassador in London of the 'indefatigable activity displayed by English travellers to spread disquiet among the people of central Asia, and to carry agitation even into the heart of the countries bordering on our frontier', at the same time as Lord Auckland, Governor General of India, was talking of his intention 'to raise up an insurmountable and, I hope, lasting barrier to all encroachments from the Westward, and to establish a base for the extension and maintenance of British influence throughout Central Asia'. Clearly the mutual distrust had given mere perceptions real substance, and as the British advanced towards Afghanistan so the Russians progressively gobbled up the independent Islamic states of central Asia. These last sentiments from Nesselrode and Auckland date to the time of the First Anglo-Afghan War, and we are getting ahead of ourselves. But the physical intervention of the British in Afghanistan in 1839, when it came, was an entirely predictable culmination of British strategic thought in the early nineteenth century.

The earliest British visitors to Bamiyan might seem at first sight only tangentially related to these bigger strategic movements. Indeed one could hardly imagine few less threatening figures than a vet and a naked Church of England clergyman. The very first Europeans to set eyes upon Bamiyan were William Moorcroft and his companions George Trebeck and George Guthrie in August 1824. Moorcroft, a veterinary surgeon by training, led a huge, slow-moving caravan laden with British-manufactured goods and was, at least theoretically, en route to secure fresh bloodstock for the East India Company's horse stud, of which he was an egregiously absentee manager. Over the course of a series of journeys to territories north of India, however, that aim had become subordinated (in Moorcroft's mind at least) to the need to counter Russian influence in central Asia. Moorcroft was a hawk before his time, hence the British manufactures which Moorcroft hoped would supplant Russian goods in Bokhara and open up central Asia to British commerce and civilising influence; hence also the urgent messages he sent to the

British authorities in Calcutta about the Russian threat he saw at every turn, and the copious notes he took as he travelled. In total this journey, Moorcroft's last, stretched from 1819 to 1825, ending with his death and those of Trebeck and Guthrie, all apparently of disease, in what is now northern Afghanistan. He died having failed in practically every element of his mission, and, disowned by Calcutta, his greatest legacy is probably the European fashion for cashmere shawls (the result of an earlier visit to Kashmir). But at Bamiyan, at least, he distinguished himself among early Western visitors by recognising the religious affiliation of the statues. On an earlier journey Moorcroft had visited Tibet, and could now convey his 'own conviction … that Bamian … was the residence of a great Lama, bearing the same relation to the Lamaism of the west, as Lhassa does now to that of the east'. He rejects the idea that the Buddhas are male and female, and argues plausibly that the popular name of the smaller Buddha, 'Shah-muma', is a corruption of 'Shak-muni' (i.e. Shakyamuni, a name of the historical Buddha). Interestingly, both Moorcroft and Elphinstone, who had described the Buddhas from afar (but was also inclined to follow informed opinion that thought them 'connected with the worship of Boodh'), refer to them as the 'celebrated idols', which suggests how rapidly Bamiyan had secured a central place on the British mental map. In Moorcroft's case Bamiyan was the more familiar for the remarkable journey of reconnaissance undertaken by his servant Mir Izzet Ullah, who in 1812 was sent ahead of Moorcroft to Tibet via Kashmir, thence into central Asia and back to India through Balkh, Bamiyan and Kabul. His account, translated into English, was published in the *Quarterly Oriental Magazine* of Calcutta in 1825, just as Moorcroft's own expedition was reaching its unfortunate conclusion. When republished in 1843, in the *Journal of the Royal Asiatic Society*, the section of his narrative including Bamiyan is omitted, since 'it has been so frequently travelled since his time, and is now so well known, that it were superfluous to continue his itinerary further'.

Moorcroft left another kind of mark at Bamiyan, for when Charles Masson was investigating the caves above the larger Buddha in 1832, 'we saw the names written with charcoal of W. MOORCROFT, W. [*sic*] TREBECK and G. GUTHRIE'. Charles Masson, as we shall see, was inspired to compose his own graffito, but it was the only writing of Moorcroft he will have seen before he left Afghanistan. Moorcroft and Trebeck's notes did not appear until 1841, edited by Horace Hayman Wilson, an academic with an authentically academic talent for rendering an inherently exciting narrative dull. (I know what a hostage to fortune that last sentence is.) By that time, anyhow, there was only one account of Afghanistan, and of Bamiyan, that everyone was talking about, and that was by Alexander Burnes.

But meanwhile, there was the naked clergyman. When the Reverend Joseph Wolff emerged from the Aq Rabat Pass, he was an apparition indeed. Wolff was at the best of times 'a strange and most curious looking man … His face is very flat … his complexion that of dough … His grey eyes roll and start, and fix themselves, at times most fearfully,' according to a contemporary; and he had a character to match, a gesticulating, incorrigibly argumentative man with peculiar yet unshakeable convictions that he expressed in a 'deep and impressive' bass or, when he was particularly excited, 'a most curious treble'. The mission that brought him to Afghanistan in 1832 was commensurately eccentric: a German Jewish convert to Christianity, ultimately Anglicanism, he was seeking the Lost Tribes of Israel with a view to converting them: 'Bokhara and Balkh are very much in my mind,' he informed his spectacularly tolerant wife, 'for I think I shall find there the Ten Tribes.' But as Wolff approached Bamiyan in April of that year the effect will have been compounded by the fact that the missionary was also stark naked. At Duab his use for himself of the title Hajji – properly applied to someone who has made the pilgrimage to Mecca – had nearly got him burned alive. Instead he was stripped of everything he carried with him, and it was in this condition, 'like Adam and Eve, without even an apron of leaves', that Wolff passed through Bamiyan. Francis Wilford might have considered that most appropriate.

Wolff was due some luck, and (although he attributed it to 'Jesus Christ my Saviour, who never left a prayer of mine unheard') it assumed the all-too-human form of Alexander Burnes. Burnes and his companions (the sickly Dr Gerard, a surveyor Muhammad Ali and the secretary and fixer par excellence Mohan Lal) happened, at the very moment that Wolff was making his chilly way from Bokhara to India, to be heading in the opposite direction. The upshot of Burnes's journey, his three-volume *Travels into Bokhara*, was an instant bestseller (shifting an astonishing 900 copies on the first day of publication), and, in the words of Peter Hopkirk, 'brought to the reader for the first time the romance, mystery and excitement of Central Asia'. Even before the book was published, Burnes's journey had made him a hero (and inflated his ego); he had been awarded the gold medal of the Royal Geographical Society, invited to join the Athenaeum, and granted a

21. Alexander 'Bokhara' Burnes, the most glamorous of the Western visitors to Bamiyan in the nineteenth century. Author of the bestselling *Travels into Bokhara* and something of a sex symbol in his day, his failure to control his own sexual appetite may have contributed to his violent death, lynched by a Kabuli mob in 1841.

private audience with William IV. Burnes was a central figure in Britain's unhappy first involvement in Afghanistan, and a flawed character in many ways: vain, unprincipled and with an unbridled sexual appetite. But he had a flair for writing, and *Travels into Bokhara* catapulted Afghanistan and central Asia, Bamiyan included, into the broader British consciousness. More immediately, Burnes was able to send Wolff some clothes and a horse from Kabul.

Burnes and his companions reached Bamiyan in May 1832, to be followed just a few months later by the most impressive and intrepid of the nineteenth-century European visitors to Afghanistan, Charles Masson. Burnes, Gerard, Lal and Masson all wrote down their impressions of the place, managing in every case, it is fair to say, to complicate rather than clarify its purpose: only Gerard is inclined to think the site is Buddhist, for example. Both Burnes and Masson provide images of the Buddhas for the first time, but the most important thing they do is convey the intense excitement generated by this place, ultimately traceable back to Wilford's words three decades previously. In the case of Burnes especially, it was a matter also of communicating this excitement to a wide reading public in Britain. 'There are no relics of Asiatic antiquity which have roused the curiosity of the learned more than the gigantic idols of Bameean,' is Burnes's opening, while Masson, who had travelled up to Bamiyan with the forces of a deeply unsavoury warlord, Hajji Khan Kakar, describes his state of mind when he arrived at Bamiyan especially vividly:

We were encamped at Bamiyan opposite to the idols and caves, so much the objects of European curiosity. I was aware of the importance attaching to them, and that the late Colonel Tod had

affirmed, that 'in the cave temples of Bamian inscriptions might
be met with; and were but the single fact established that the
colossal figures in the temple were Buddhist, it would be worth
a journey. Perhaps no spot in the world is more curious than this
region.'

To James Tod, an authority on Indian antiquities (and
yet another surveyor), is generally attributed the rediscovery of the Greek presence in India, research that Masson
would advance dramatically among the Buddhist remains
near Kabul and Jalalabad. But at Bamiyan both Masson and
Burnes failed to recognise what they were looking at, Burnes
speculating that 'we owe the idols of Bameean to the caprice
of some person of rank, who … sought for an immortality in
the colossal images', while Masson comments to similar effect,
'We visited Bamian under the idea of meeting with Buddhist
antiquities, but it became evident that they were of another
character,' the dynastic burial place of a race of Iranian kings,
he supposed, the colossal Buddhas being images of two of
them. It weighed heavily with Masson that he could see none
of the stupas so familiar to him from elsewhere. The prickly
antiquarian suffered other disappointments. An unfortunate
inhabitant of a cave at the base of the 55m Buddha suffered
the rough edge of Charles Masson's tongue when he was
trying to locate a stairway in the niche wall equivalent to that
near the smaller Buddha:

The superior idol has or had the same facilities of ascent to the
summit, but at the time of our visit the lower caves near it were
occupied by an unaccommodating Tajik, who had stowed in the
passage his stock of provender. We could not prevail on him by

*menace or entreaty to open the path, and he evasively affirmed
that he had never heard of one.*

That poor householder was only telling the truth, and one can't help but sympathise with him, invaded without warning by a foreign stranger with rudimentary Persian insisting that his house had a back door. Masson thought he had found a key to the character of Bamiyan in an inscription (he thought it was Pahlavi, the script of pre-Islamic Persia) which he still managed to spy at the summit of the niche of the larger Buddha, directly above its head. Others were not convinced it was even script at all. It remains a fundamental problem for historians of Bamiyan that no inscriptions survive to identify its founders or rulers. Yet Masson, as we have seen, did find a more recent inscription, the names of Moorcroft and his equally ill-fated companions in the caves above the larger Buddha. He was clearly inspired, since twentieth-century French archaeologists found in the same area of caves the following graffito: 'If any fool this high samootch [cave] explore,/ Know Charles Masson has been here before.' Masson's name alone has been found elsewhere in the vicinity. Today, unfortunately, the urge to write names on the archaeological remains of Bamiyan, so frustratingly resisted by the people who constructed it in the first place, has run riot, caves full of a scribbled *yadgari* ('woz 'ere') followed by the names of the Hizb-i Wahdat or Taliban fighters who passed through.

Burnes's companion Dr Gerard, as we saw in Chapter 2, responded in a rather disturbed way to the Buddha cliff. He was also convinced that the Buddhas were made of mud rather than solid rock, but on the other hand thought they probably were, on balance, Buddhas. He also claimed to have evidence that the Russians were taking an interest in Bamiyan: 'A Persian of our party, who had been at Moscow, had drawings of the idols, which he affirmed were an object of enquiry in that country … ; and when they send to Bokhara for coins and other antiquities, there is nothing surprising in their extending research to Bameán.' The Buddhas certainly very soon became a talking point for the European intelligentsia. We have seen no less a personage than Goethe (as early as 1819) condemning them as representative examples of Indian idolatry, far inferior to the religious genius of Persia. But the value of reading today the discussion of Bamiyan by the great German geographer Carl Ritter in 1838 – which could count as the first truly scholarly account of Bamiyan – is, rather as with the accounts of Burnes and Masson, more than anything to gain a sense of the intense intellectual excitement that the place, and the accounts of its visitors, generated in academic circles. Ritter had clearly immersed himself in the flood of material being published in travel memoirs and articles in the *Journal of the Asiatic Society of Bengal* (the successor to *Asiatick Researches*), Burnes's writing especially, and in some respects (for example, his awareness of Xuanzang, although he didn't know about the pilgrim's visit to Bamiyan itself) he is much better informed than the visitors. (Academics like Ritter and H. H. Wilson were generally some way ahead of the men on the ground, utterly clear that the site was Buddhist, for example.) But Ritter nevertheless indulges in a game of intercultural join-the-dots almost as potty as Wilford's: he identifies Bamiyan with the cave of Mani, founder of the religion Manichaeism; the location of Alexander's foundation Alexandria ad Caucasum; and the cave which Alexander's Macedonian soldiers had identified as the place where

Prometheus had been chained, and Heracles had come to free him. But Wilford and Ritter weren't alone in wanting to give Bamiyan this kind of central role in world history, as we shall see. To the Romantic sensibility especially, Bamiyan was such an exciting place that it just had to have a commensurate significance.

INFORMATION, INFORMATION, INFORMATION

Burnes and Masson are representative figures in this story in other respects. Burnes would die during the British occupation of Afghanistan in 1841, but Masson in his way was just as caught up in the process that led to war. Both, for a start, were spies, though one much more willingly than the other, and both embodied the thirst for information which turned antiquarians like Masson into spies, and spies like Burnes into antiquarians. Information was the currency of British strategic thinking: as the future Governor General Lord Ellenborough wrote to Sir John Malcolm, perhaps the greatest influence on British foreign policy in India, 'What we ought to have is *Information*. The first, the second and the third thing a government ought always to have is *Information*.' But to explain how thoroughly political the nineteenth-century interest in Bamiyan was, we need to introduce another character, Claude Martine Wade.

Wade never went to Bamiyan, but he knew a lot of people who had. He 'was a short, fat man fond of eating and sleeping' (Yapp), and probably also on the take. But he was at the same time one of the most powerful men in India, 'acute, knowledgeable, and prickly'. Wade was one of the class of 'Politicals' who drove British policy in India, in particular nudging the frontier further and further across the north of the country. He was based at Ludhiana, on the River Sutlej at the edge of the territory ruled by the great Sikh Ranjit Singh. From Ludhiana, Wade had an effective monopoly on that precious commodity, information, emerging from Ranjit's kingdom and from further afield – and a perceived authority in interpreting it. Like any official, Wade sought professional advancement, and at this critical point on British India's north-west frontier, Wade's personal motivations had a way of transmogrifying into British strategy. The personal thus becomes terrifyingly political in the story of British expansion, but there is also a fascinating lack of distinction between political and non-political information. Wade was greedy for intelligence about the inadequately understood territories beyond the Sutlej, Ranjit's Punjab, and Afghanistan beyond. But Wade's intelligence gathering unselfconsciously mixes the overtly political and the academic.

A representative example of this might be found in the *Journal of the Asiatic Society of Bengal*, which in 1836 published an article titled 'Conjectures on the March of Alexander', by Monsieur Court, 'former student of the military academy of St Cyr'. Court simultaneously published in the *Journal Asiatique* in Paris, and was in fact General Claude-Auguste Court, one of a number of European soldiers, many of them unemployed Napoleonic veterans, who travelled east to serve Ranjit Singh in his project to raise his army in the Punjab to European standards (which, with the British camped on the Sutlej, can only have seemed sensible). It is noticeable that, once in India, old Napoleonic-era enmities evaporate. For instance, General Court is the author of a touchingly concerned letter of advice, notwithstanding sweeping generalisations about 'les Orientaux', which he gave to Alexander Burnes as the latter left Lahore, Ranjit's capital, on his way to Afghanistan and Bokhara. Ranjit Singh himself was clear that there was no distinction to be drawn between Westerners: 'German, French or English, all these European bastards are alike,' he once perceptively remarked. The topic of Court's article represents another shared interest of Europeans on the northwest frontier, for they were, almost to a man, obsessed with Alexander the Great. But one of the most telling features of General Court's submission is the subheading under the title and author: '[Communicated by Captain C. M. Wade]'. The 'Information, information, information' that the British authorities desired, and that Politicals such as Wade were keen to have the credit of providing, encompassed antiquities as much as contemporary material, especially when the antiquities were so closely tied to routes and the lie of the land.

Another illustration of the proximity, indeed inseparability, of espionage and archaeology in Afghanistan is the story of how Wade recruited Charles Masson. Masson was of considerable interest to Wade, and probably had been for some time, seemingly ever since the American adventurer Josiah Harlan had informed Wade about a suspicious Westerner, Masson, whom he had encountered en route to Kabul in 1827. In reality Charles Masson was James Lewis, a soldier who had deserted from the Bengal Horse Artillery, a capital crime, and fled British jurisdiction. Thereafter, changing his name and masquerading as an American from Kentucky, 'Masson' excavated Buddhist sites and amassed an enormous coin collection, detailing his discoveries in the *Journal of the Asiatic Society of Bengal* – of which, as we already know, Wade was an avid reader. In 1834 Wade set out his thinking in a letter to a superior. Masson was without doubt a deserter, and desertion 'is a crime which is viewed I believe by our government with a degree of rigour that scarcely ever admits of pardon'. Nevertheless Wade hoped that he might be forgiven communications he had already had with Masson, and be repaid for any sums he might in the future pass to him to encourage him in his activities, given 'his acknowledged talent and ability and the light which his interesting researches are likely to throw on the ancient history, antiquities and present state of Afghanistan'. Masson's knowledge of Afghanistan was unparalleled, as Wade insisted, and the value of such knowledge outweighed the desire for exemplary punishment of a deserter. In 1835 Masson, or rather Lewis, received a free pardon, and by that time Masson was Wade's creature, 'Agent in Cabul for communicating intelligence of the state of affairs in that quarter on a salary of Rs.250 per mensem,' and restricted by his new obligations and the suspicions his new role provoked among his Afghan contacts in his ability to pursue his beloved researches on the ground. Implicated in the increasingly convoluted intrigues of the British in Afghanistan, Masson eventually had to leave a country he loved in 1838, never to return. Burnes returned with an invading army the following year, as the British attempted to ensure a sympathetic regime in Kabul by deposing the existing Amir, Dost Muhammad, and replacing him with Shah Shuja. Burnes's death in Kabul on 2 November 1841, ripped apart by a mob, was one of the events that led to an infamous massacre of British and Indian troops and camp-followers as they retreated from Kabul to Jalalabad. All in all, it is understandable that Afghan authorities came to assume that an English archaeologist was an English spy, and that when they decided to invite foreign experts to investigate the remarkable archaeological legacy of their country, it was to the French they turned.

One more thing that Masson and Burnes had in common, to set against their manifold differences (Masson utterly deplored the developments in British policy that led to the First Anglo-Afghan War, and the purposes to which his own intelligence had been put; Burnes was always ready to cut his cloth in the furtherance of his career), is a fundamental educational conditioning that they shared with practically all the European visitors in this period. One regularly gets the impression when reading about Wade's dealings with Harlan, or Harlan's with Masson, or Masson's with Burnes, that classicists are talking to classicists; that the pleasure of the meeting goes further than the opportunity to speak to someone whose native language is one's own. What the well-educated functionaries of empire also shared was an education centred upon the ancient world, and as soldiers or former soldiers in a predominantly military environment, there is one classical figure above all who inspired their interest: Alexander of Macedon. The further the British progressed into the northwest of India, the more they encountered territory familiar to them from stirring accounts of Alexander's campaigns in the fourth century BC. For men such as General Court, the Punjab in which they found themselves could not fail to evoke Alexander's progress, and his fascination for the topic is reflected in that article for the *Journal of the Asiatic Society of Bengal*. But these men saw Alexander *everywhere*. The real pleasure of encountering other Europeans consisted in the common cultural points of reference of men who know their Quintus Curtius – and are quite possibly carrying in their jacket pockets, even in the middle of Afghanistan, copies of his *Histories of Alexander the Great*.

Afghanistan was not the first place to be identified as a frontier against hostile influence. Indeed, if one listened to all the opinions of British agents eager to make a name for themselves, to borrow another felicitous turn of phrase from Yapp, 'the keys of India were as plentiful as fallen leaves in autumn; the door they were intended to unlock was not that of India but of promotion'. A popular candidate for a frontier to British India before the Hindu Kush was the great river Indus, but Yapp suspects another motivation for what became a British fixation with this river: 'No one, reading the works of the frontier travellers, can avoid remarking upon the way in which the scenes they observed recalled their classical education. In this context the Indus acquired a romantic attraction which added to the force of its appeal.' In essence, the Europeans had reached a place where the presence of one of their own, Alexander the Great, was tangible. Almost all these Europeans were would-be Alexanders; some succumbed to the fantasy more severely than others. Alexander Burnes enjoyed and exploited the coincidence of his given name, and here describes his reaction to the Indus, up which he travelled in 1831 to deliver a gift of five English shire horses to the ruler of the Punjab, Ranjit Singh, at Lahore. The real reason, needless to say, was to secure information about the river, its navigability in particular:

It is difficult to describe the enthusiasm one feels on first behold-
ing the scenes which have exercised the genius of Alexander. That

22. Lieut. Vincent Eyre, author of *The Military Operations at Cabul*. This
was a critical account of the conduct of the First Anglo-Afghan War which
also included the journal Eyre had kept during his time as a captive of the
Afghans from January to September 1842. The plight of the captives, who
also included Eyre's wife and son, gripped the British public, and Eyre's
account was another publishing sensation, enlivened by his drawings of
scenes from his captivity and fellow captives.

*hero has reaped the immortality which he so much desired, and
transmitted the history of his conquests, allied with his name, to
posterity. A town or a river, which lies on his route, has acquired
a celebrity that time serves only to increase; and, while we gaze
on the Indus, we connect ourselves, at least in association, with
the ages of distant glory.*

Josiah Harlan had a bigger Alexander-fixation than
anyone. When he saw the Indus, he was intensely moved:

*To look for the first time upon the furthest stream that had
borne upon its surface the world's victor two thousand years ago.
To gaze upon the landscape he had viewed. To tread upon the
earth where Alexander bled. To stand upon that spot where the
wounded hero knelt exhausted when pierced by the arrows of the
barbarians.*

There's an odd but critical paradox here. We have already
seen Mountstuart Elphinstone at the Indus, pondering the
inaccessible wonders beyond the mountains in Afghanistan. Masson too found himself on the banks of the same
river, 'reflecting on the people and scenes I was about to leave
behind, and on the unknown lands and races the passage of the
river would open to my observation'. The appeal of Afghanistan, and Bamiyan as the encapsulation of Afghanistan, lay
largely in its mystery, that enticing terra incognita. Yet it is an
unfamiliar place that its European explorers feel a deep psychological compulsion to make familiar, no longer in terms of
biblical history but in terms of an equally powerful Western
discourse, classical learning – in other words, by mapping onto
it the exploits of the greatest European cultural icon.

There is a moving passage in the diary (with illustrations) of Lieutenant Vincent Eyre, who with his wife and young son was part of the dreadful retreat of the Kabul contingent of the British forces during the First Anglo-Afghan War in January 1842, an event which might be seen as the ultimate, tragic upshot of British interest in Afghanistan in the first half of the nineteenth century. Eyre was already seriously wounded, but now the column of British and Indian soldiers and camp followers was attacked from all sides as it withdrew through the narrow passes on the way to Jalalabad in freezing conditions. Eyre and his family were lucky enough to be taken hostage, the start of nine months in captivity: among their fellow captives were Lady Sale and her daughter Alexandrina Sturt, whose husband, responsible for that tranquil drawing of Shahr-i Zohak, died in agony of an abdominal wound the day they were taken. Four months later, in spring, Eyre describes walking back towards Kabul along the route of the retreat. It is an exhausting journey, made appalling by the sight and stench of the unburied corpses of those killed in January: Sturt, according to Eyre, had been 'the only man of the whole force who received Christian burial'. But 24 May offers some relief:

> *Again on the move at 9 A.M. The Khoord Cabul pass being now absolutely impassable from the stench of dead bodies, we took the direct road to Cabul, having Alexander the Great's column in view nearly the whole way ... we halted for half an hour at a deliciously cool and clear spring, which supplied a small tank or pond: just above this, crowning the hill to the left, stood a ruined Grecian tope [stupa]. Resuming our way, we again entered some hills, the road making a continuous ascent for about a couple*

23. A 'Prison Scene' by Vincent Eyre. As this picture implies, the greatest enemy of the captives was not the primitive conditions so much as the intense boredom; though we have that boredom in part to thank for the richly detailed journals kept by a number of captives. The woman and child in this picture are Eyre's wife, Emily, and his son.

of miles to Alexander's pillar, one of the most ancient relics of antiquity in the East, and conspicuously situated on the crest of a mountain range which bounds the plain of Cabul on the southeast. It stands about seventy feet high; the shaft is of the Doric order, standing on a cubic pedestal, and surmounted by a sort of urn. As we reached this classic spot, a view of almost unrivalled magnificence burst suddenly upon our sight. At the distance of some two thousand feet below, the whole picturesque and highly cultivated valley of Cabul was spread before us like a map; the towering ranges of Kohistan and Hindoo Khoosh, clad in a pure vesture of snow, bounded the horizon, at the distance of nearly a hundred miles.

The refreshing spring and the uplifting view to the mountains are clearly a balm on Eyre's troubled soul: we get little hint here of what another captive described as a road 'rugged in the extreme, and very steep'. But so, equally clearly, is the column he sees and domesticates with the names and classical orders of his education, and with a very elegant sketch. (Sturt had also drawn it.) This column, the Minar-i Chakari, has since become another victim of Afghan history, though less deliberately than the Buddhas of Bamiyan. Weakened by damage suffered during the Soviet occupation, it collapsed without further assistance in March 1998. The column was probably, like the stupas in the vicinity, originally associated with a Buddhist monastery, and like the stupas again, a symbol of Buddhahood – thus, like the Buddhas, it was only very indirectly associated with the campaigns of Alexander. The name of Alexander became attached to it in local tradition, which also called it Minar-i Sikandar, it seems, but it became familiar to the British during their occupation of Kabul, a

24. The Minar-i Chakari or Minar-i Sikandar, Column of Alexander, which stood until 1998 on a mountain ridge 16km south-east of Kabul. During the British occupation of Kabul in the First Anglo-Afghan War, we are told, 'parties were sometimes made by gentlemen to visit it'. Its supposed connection to Alexander intrigued Western visitors, and a number of drawings of it from the period survive.

time of hunting, horse-racing and amateur theatricals among the dangerously naïve British community, when we learn that 'parties were sometimes made by gentlemen to visit it'. The false sense of security felt by the British in Afghanistan in 1841 notoriously contributed to their undoing, encouraging them to reduce their forces to an inadequate level and locate what remained in indefensible positions – and to bring their wives and families to join them in Kabul. We might speculate how much their classical educations contributed to that disastrous misconception that Afghanistan could be a familiar and safe place for European interlopers.

We encounter Lieutenant Eyre in an optimistic frame of mind again on 5 September, sitting on the head of the 38m Buddha. By this time he and the rest of the surviving captives had been moved to Bamiyan by their Afghan guards as a British 'Army of Retribution' closed on Kabul. From Bamiyan, at the edge of Afghan territory, they could readily be shifted across the mountains to Turkistan: and that meant slavery. It was a tense time, their quarters at Bamiyan especially primitive and their prospects grim, and desperate efforts were being made to buy over the guards before it was too late. In Britain, meanwhile, the fate of these hostages dominated public opinion in a way that has been compared to the American hostage crisis in Iran in 1979–81. On their eventual release (secured in the main by the brave and resourceful Mohan Lal), the former captives, especially the tough-as-nails Lady Florentia Sale, were fêted, their release a substitute victory. 'Captivity!/ Thy thralls are free;/ Britons have nought to do with thee', ran one triumphal paraphrase of *Rule Britannia*. To high and low in Victorian society Lady Sale became a household name. A satirical take in *Punch* on the 1845 Summer Exhibition at the Royal Academy describes the society portraitist James Sant's *A Portrait of Lady Sale*, 'with whom we had become familiar at ASTLEY'S'. A circus performance at Astley's Amphitheatre had retold the ordeal of the hostages, culminating in the scene which 'drew down the loudest praise': 'The heroic manner in which she fought the double sword combat with six Afghans, whom she put to flight.' (I like to think that the scenery of this London circus performance included representations of the Buddhas of Bamiyan.) Subsequently the journals that Lady Sale and Vincent Eyre had kept became publishing sensations to compare with Burnes's *Travels into Bokhara*, accompanied by 'Lieutenant V. Eyre's sketches of the CABUL PRISON-ERS: 30 Plates, lithographed by Lowes Dickinson, in a form adapted to bind up with Lady Sale's Journal and Lieutenant Eyre's Narrative': three images, the concluding three, are of Bamiyan, one for each of the Buddhas and a fold-out panorama of the cliff face. But on 5 September Eyre had found some peace, and Alexander again had had a lot to do with it:

I ascended to the top of the female image by a series of stairs and galleries, the labour of excavating which through the solid rock must have been immense. From the main gallery others branched off in all directions, communicating with distant chambers. While sitting on the lady's crown, enjoying a splendid view of the country, I was joined by some of the inhabitants, who were very inquisitive to know what was written in our books concerning the place. I told them it was generally supposed that Alexander the Great founded a city there. His name is diffused so generally among all classes in Affghanistan, that I was pretty certain my information would prove satisfactory. After a long chat on late

25. Lady Florentia Sale, the 'Grenadier in Petticoats' fêted in Britain as a heroine on her release from captivity. Her memoirs, *Journal of the Disasters in Affghanistan*, were another bestseller, and her courage was immortalized in society portraits and in circus performances. She shared her captivity with her recently widowed daughter Alexandrina Sturt, who presented Lady Sale with a granddaughter, Julia Florentia, while they were confined in Kabul. Alexandrina was killed in the Indian Mutiny in 1857; it is good to report that Julia Florentia Mulock, née Sturt, Lady Sale's granddaughter, born in captivity in Afghanistan, whose mother was murdered the day before her fifteenth birthday, died peacefully at Wincanton in Somerset in 1910.

events, these men assured me that the whole population of the valley were favourable to the English, whose rule they preferred to any other, and that all the chiefs were most anxious we should be released and peace be restored.

In actual fact, Alexander's connection with Bamiyan was at best fleeting. But most of the nineteenth-century visitors to Bamiyan were determined to identify Bamiyan with the city, Alexandria ad Caucasum, which Alexander had founded early in 329 BC before crossing the Hindu Kush into Bactria, and to which he eventually returned in the summer of 327, prior to launching his invasion of India. His army *may* have followed the route via Bamiyan and the Shibar Pass on his return, but even that is by no means certain. Others, including Masson and the leading academic authority of the time, H. H. Wilson, placed this Alexandria (there were many, many others) at the confluence of the Ghurband and Panjshir rivers near modern Bagram, north of Kabul, controlling two significant routes over the Hindu Kush, and that is the modern view. When Eyre places Alexandria at Bamiyan, he is reflecting the view of a strong constituency, but what we are really looking at is a special instance of the European compulsion to find Alexander, an equally strong impulse to associate with Alexander the most celebrated site in Afghanistan, which by general consent was Bamiyan. Perhaps the psychology is best illustrated by Godfrey Thomas Vigne, a remarkable phenomenon in 1830s Afghanistan in that he genuinely seems to have travelled there for pleasure, with no hint of ulterior political motives. But Vigne was still a product of his time and superior education (at Harrow), and hence the peculiar exchange we find in Vigne's *A Personal Narrative of a Visit to Ghuzni, Kabul, and Afghanistan* between the author and the academic H. H. Wilson. Vigne was unable to get to Bamiyan, an omission he much regretted, but this doesn't stop him discussing at some length a place he never got to, and quoting in extenso a letter from Wilson, the gist of which is that Bamiyan has nothing to do with Alexander. Undeterred, and 'with the greatest possible deference to such an authority', Vigne sets out to demolish Wilson's infinitely better informed position, concluding that 'I am much inclined to think that the pretensions of Bamiyan to be the *Alexandria ad Caucasum* are far from being without foundation.' It's obvious enough here that a psychological need to locate Alexander in Bamiyan was far too great for overwhelming arguments to the contrary to carry the day.

Vincent Eyre chilling out on the 38m Buddha's head and the carefree British garrison galloping over to the Minar-i Sikandar introduce another dimension, though. Alexander was a familiar figure to the Europeans. But one of the astonishing things about Europe's favourite psychopath is how far his story had been adopted by non-Europeans. As Iskandar or Sikandar (the 'al' dropped in the Islamic world as if an Arabic definite article), Alexander had entered the folklore of Afghanistan. At Balkh in the thirteenth century Marco Polo heard about the marriage of Alexander and 'the daughter of Darius' from the locals, and in Badakhshan of kings descended from Alexander and his Bactrian bride and horses descended from Bucephalus. These stories were still alive and thriving in the nineteenth century. Indeed, the Alexander legend survived longer, and more vibrantly, in Afghan oral tradition than in any other part of the world except Greece itself. In Hindu India, on the other hand, such traditions were less in evidence, so in effect, as the British progressed north-west, they not only started to encounter territory familiar from European accounts of Alexander, but a familiar mental landscape and symbolic language, people who seemed to share Western cultural reference points such as Alexander.

ALEXANDER THE CHRISTIAN

One of the most brilliant analyses of the imperial mindset is Rudyard Kipling's short story 'The Man Who Would Be King', in which two British chancers, Daniel Dravot and Peachey Carnehan, temporarily carve out a kingdom for themselves in Afghanistan, by exploiting the memory of Alexander and what turn out to be the roots of Masonic ritual among the pagan inhabitants of Kafiristan. In particular Kipling spears the imperial fantasy, especially true of the British encounter with Afghanistan and especially acute when Bamiyan becomes Alexandria, that the colonised people are really just like us. Here Danny Dravot meets the Kafir leaders:

> *Then he asks them about their villages, and learns that they was fighting one against the other, and were sick and tired of it. And when they wasn't doing that they was fighting with the Mohammedans. 'You can fight those when they come into our country,' says Dravot. 'Tell off every tenth man of your tribes for a Frontier guard, and send two hundred at a time to this valley to be drilled. Nobody is going to be shot or speared any more so long as he does well, and I know that you won't cheat me, because you're white people – sons of Alexander – and not like common, black Mohammedans. You are* my *people, and by God,' says he, running off into English at the end – 'I'll make a damned fine Nation of you, or I'll die in the making!'*

The notion that the non-Islamic people of Kafiristan ('Land of the Unbelievers': after they were forcibly converted in the later nineteenth century, the province was renamed Nuristan, 'Land of Light') were descended from Greek soldiers is persistent: in the last decade the *Spectator* has sponsored a project to find traces of Greek or Macedonian ancestry in the DNA of Afghans, without much success. It has been suggested, again not awfully plausibly, that the model for Kipling's adventurers in Afghanistan was Josiah Harlan, the American who exposed Charles Masson. (If modelled on anything, the great archetype of false confidence followed by catastrophe is the British disaster of 1841–2.) Ben Macintyre, in his splendid biography of Harlan, *Josiah the Great*, has done as much for this distinctly unsavoury character as could be done, but he remains a man of easy loyalties, prepared to serve either party within Afghanistan, or Ranjit Singh, or the British, or indeed the Russians, to whom he also apparently tried to sell his knowledge of the mountain passes of Afghanistan. This singularly unprincipled individual nevertheless convinced himself that he was a civilising force comparable to his great model and inspiration, Alexander, and his Alexander fantasy was at its strongest in 1838–9, as he led an Afghan army via Bamiyan on a punitive expedition against the Khan of Qunduz, the notorious slave-dealer Murad Beg, along a route he describes, and feels deeply, as, 'the route of Alexander the Great to the province of Bulkh, the Bactria of ancient times'. For Harlan the blessings bestowed by Alexander could be encapsulated by a piece of ancient jewellery he had picked up:

I have now before me an engraved gem … The figure represents

Minerva standing on the prow of a boat, armed with helmet, shield, and spear … The bold and scientific address skilfully exhibited in the execution of the engraving, the polish of the gem, the voluminous design of the representation, indicate the arts, the sciences, the commerce, war, and letters predominant twenty-two centuries ago in the heart of Asia, implanted there by a European philanthropist … In seven years Alexander performed feats that have consecrated his memory amongst the benefactors of mankind, and impressed the stamp of civilisation on the face of the known world, which have commemorated his labours amongst the blessings of a Deity.

One of a string of questions put to the Reverend Joseph Wolff by the capricious and murderous Amir of Bokhara during his second visit to this central-Asian khanate was, Why do the English people like old coins? Wolff, playing a commendably straight bat, answered that coins 'were the great guides of the historian in determining his eras, and formed a metallic history of the earth'. But the Amir's question was more penetrating than that. The European visitors to central Asia, Russians included, were fascinated by ancient coins, as they were by classical gems like Harlan's, as tangible relics of that seemingly familiar, Greek-speaking Afghanistan that at some level they aspired to recreate, and the British Museum was a particular beneficiary of collections such as the enormous one amassed by Masson. Three albums of rubbings of General Court's extensive coin collection turned up in a British book sale in 1994, allowing many of Court's coins, which had also made their way to the British Museum, to be identified as such. Subscribers to the *Journal of the Asiatic Society of Bengal* in 1840 could read a submission by one Captain William Hay,

dated 7 April 1840, on a copper coin of the Greek king Deme-
trius, 'discovered in digging some trenches at Bameean', and
another coin of Euthydemus, the Greek inscription of which
is of course competently analysed by the Captain. From a
caravan passing through Bamiyan from Balkh, Hay picked
up two more Indo-Greek coins. The gem with the image of
Minerva, bringer of the arts of civilisation, is used by Harlan
to contrast Alexander's supposedly benign imperialism (and
by implication, Harlan's own) with that of the British, whose
invasion in 1839 had curtailed Harlan's career in Afghanistan.
But in this respect Harlan and the British (and the French,
Germans, Swiss) had once again more in common than Harlan
cared to admit. When he returned to the United States, he
was something of a celebrity, greeted by a gushing piece in
the *United States Gazette* which enthusiastically picked up on
Harlan's self-identification with Alexander as it describes the
campaign which took him twice through Bamiyan, the second
time (we may recall from Chapter 2) leading forces that pil-
laged and brutalised the local population:

> *We view this expedition as altogether unique since the period of*
> *Alexander's conquests. With this prominent exception, no Chris-*
> *tian chief of European descent ever penetrated so far into the*
> *interior of Central Asia under circumstances so peculiar as char-*
> *acterize General Harlan's enterprise, and we relinquish the palm*
> *of antecedent honour to the Macedonian hero alone. Retracing*
> *the steps of Alexander, General Harlan has performed a feat that*
> *ranks with the passage of the Simplon … This expedition may*
> *be viewed as a pioneering effort to prove the existence of a prac-*
> *ticable military passage between Cabul and Bulkh, the ancient*
> *Bactra.*

Most telling of all here, surely, is the journalistic slip that makes Alexander the Great (d.323 BC) a Christian. It is true that Alexander dominated the restricted perspective of the first European visitors to Bamiyan. If we wanted to be very reductive indeed, we could regard the nineteenth century, very obviously in the case of Francis Wilford, but implicitly also with the other European responses to Bamiyan, as the Christian West's turn to attempt to accommodate to their world view this outlandish wonder.

5

....

BAMIYAN, ITS FUTURE AND
ITS PAST

Those phenomena which arise from a cause,
The Tathagata declared what is their cause
And what is their cessation.
Thus the great Mendicant has spoken.

The ye dharma formula

Western visitors to Bamiyan declined after the First Anglo-Afghan War, and it was only in the aftermath of a second conflict between the British and the Afghans, in 1878–81, that Britons returned there. They were surveyors and geographers again, predictably, serving one of a series of Afghan Boundary Commissions, which between 1883 and 1905 had the task of drawing a clear line between Afghanistan and the Russian Empire, and thus between Russian and British spheres of influence, the indeterminacy of which had caused such grief in the course of the nineteenth century. But they took the opportunity to explore as much of Afghanistan as the government would allow, and the result was, in the words of Warwick Ball, 'the most thorough and comprehensive information gathering exercise ever undertaken on Afghanistan', yielding among many other things the first accurate measurements of the Buddhas of Bamiyan, as we saw in Chapter 1. A report in *The Times* from January 1887 records Captain P. J. Maitland's effusive response to Bamiyan ('to see these antiquities alone was worth all the trouble of the journey'), although, this being primarily an intelligence operation, he and his companion did not forget to note 'full details of the various passes leading over the main range to Cabul'. One might think that by this point in time the British army already had all the information it could conceivably need about 'the various passes leading over the main range to Cabul'.

The Afghan Boundary Commissions, representatives of a foreign military surveying Afghan territory, tell us a lot about the status of Afghanistan after the Second Anglo-Afghan War. Though notionally independent of British control at this time, Afghanistan dates its true independence from 1919, after a *third* Anglo-Afghan War. But the peculiar political circumstances of Maitland's mission can launch an important thread of this concluding chapter, the fundamental question of ownership. At the end of a history characterised by attempts to claim Bamiyan by a spectrum of religious or cultural traditions, to whom does this precious archaeological site belong in 2012? The world? The Buddhists of the world? The nation of Afghanistan? The people of Bamiyan? If this critical question is answerable at all, it will only be after stopping the yawning historical gap I have left between the nineteenth century and the very start of the twenty-first.

ON THE SHOULDERS OF GIANTS

The first photograph of a Bamiyan Buddha finally appeared in *At the Court of the Amir* (1895), John Alfred Gray's memoir of his time as personal surgeon to Abdur Rahman, a ruler of Afghanistan at the end of the nineteenth century who cast a long shadow over the subsequent history of the country, and especially over that of the Hazaras, the dominant ethnic group at Bamiyan. Oddly, perhaps, the first Buddha to be recorded this way, in a photograph attributed to Arthur Collins, a geologist, was the smaller of the two, but since that time by far the majority of images have been of the 55m Buddha, the more harmoniously realised figure as well as the larger, and also, by virtue of its position, the easier of the two to photograph satisfactorily. Also somewhat surprisingly, Gray is still only tentatively attributing the figures to Buddhism. In terms of interpreting the Buddhas of Bamiyan and their surroundings a much more significant event was the visit of the French scholar Alfred Foucher and his wife to Bamiyan in November 1922, in the course of a visit to Afghanistan which also saw the establishment of what became the dominant force in twentieth-century Afghan archaeology, the Délégation archéologique française en Afghanistan (DAFA), which for many years exercised an effective monopoly over archaeological activity in the country. The favour shown to the French from the 1920s onwards in a country until recently under the oppressive influence of the British was no coincidence. Abdur Rahman's grandson Amanullah, a nationalistic and modernising ruler of Afghanistan, after securing full independence from the British in 1919, underlined his internal and external policies with measures in the cultural realm – establishing a National Museum in Kabul and reaching an agreement with foreign specialists who were emphatically not British to investigate the archaeology of the country.

One undeserving victim of Amanullah's arrangement with

the French (and embargo on the British) was Aurel Stein, the great Hungarian-British archaeologist and explorer who did more than anyone to trace the transmission of Buddhism along the 'Silk Road' through central Asia, braving numerous mountain ranges and deserts in the process. He desperately wanted to visit Afghanistan, but it was closed to him. In 1915 Stein wrote to a friend from western China, 'I have visited interesting cave shrines at Kizil, a link of importance between the "Thousand Buddhas" of Tun-huang and the caves of Bamian, north of Kabul. When may the time come for seeing that Bactrian prototype?' The time finally seemed to have come in 1943, when Stein was eighty, but having made it as far as Kabul, and visited the National Museum (then in its glorious heyday), this remarkable man caught a chill and died, first telling a friend, 'I have had a wonderful life, and it could not be concluded more happily than in Afghanistan which I have wanted to visit for sixty years.' His grave survives in the foreign cemetery in Kabul, and perhaps of all the people we have encountered in this book Stein is the one who most passionately wished, and most deserved, to set eyes upon Bamiyan. In general, nevertheless, it is hard not to sympathise with Amanullah's refusal to distinguish between British antiquarian interest and British espionage: those coin-collectors were indeed almost invariably also spies.

DAFA's discoveries in Afghanistan rank among the most exciting anywhere in the world. At Begram in the 1930s, for example, a treasure trove of artefacts was discovered, probably a merchant's store, dating to the early centuries AD, which dramatically illustrated the commercial centrality of Afghanistan in that period: items from the Mediterranean, notably sophisticated glasswork, lay alongside ivories from India and

Chinese lacquers. In the 1920s, at Hadda near Jalalabad, an enormous Buddhist site was excavated, revealing a style of stucco sculpture profoundly indebted to Greco-Roman artistic traditions – Buddhist belief expressed in a thoroughly Mediterranean idiom – while a much smaller Buddhist site at Fondukistan, in the Ghurband valley east of Bamiyan (excavated in 1937), yielded images in an entirely different style that blended influences from India, China and central Asia. Excavations of the remarkable site of Ai Khanum, a Greek city dating to the third century BC (the aftermath of Alexander's campaigns) beside the Oxus river (Amu Darya) on the northern border of Afghanistan, ended in 1978, and the subsequent Soviet invasion in 1979 brought a halt to DAFA's fieldwork for twenty years. But I have mentioned a few times the DAFA excavations in the last few years at the ancient copper-working site (and Buddhist monastic centre) of Mes Ainak. (It is an odd and hypocritical thing to say in a book with this title, but it frustrates many archaeologists of Afghanistan that Bamiyan garners most of the attention and almost all the funds: there is so much more out there to be found.) At Bamiyan DAFA's activities were comparatively superficial – three surveys and one rather hurried dig – but they possess the same nostalgic, intrepid quality as Aurel Stein in the Taklamakan Desert: a wonderful photograph survives of Jean Carl perched on the right arm of the larger Buddha, holding the ropes on which he had made his perilous descent from the shoulders and the head. Carl, an architect by training, was a close collaborator of Joseph Hackin, Foucher's successor as Director of DAFA, and his wife Ria, and became personally very attached to the couple. When news reached him in London in 1941 of their death at sea

26. The DAFA archaeologist Jean Carl during his descent of the Western Buddha in the early 1930s. He worked at Bamiyan with Joseph and Ria Hackin, and was devastated when the ship in which they were travelling was torpedoed in 1941. At the lower right of the photograph one can see the holes that held the pegs, connected by ropes, over which the folds of the Buddha's *samghati* were moulded in clay.

in a torpedo attack while serving the Free French, Carl took his own life.

Alexander the Great continued to exert a fascination over the first generation of 'proper' archaeologists in Afghanistan, guiding what they were looking for (Islamic material was not a priority for these researchers), and how they interpreted what they found. In Bamiyan one sign of Europeans still looking for the Greeks was a determination to date the Buddhas far earlier than their true date, an attempt to associate them with the great Kushan monarch Kanishka in the second century AD, and thus with a cultural environment where Greek influence was still tangible. Stein's description of them as the 'Bactrian prototype' for developments as far as China reflects the same impulse to date them early and thus attribute to Bamiyan a greater role in the transmission of Buddhism than it could rightly claim. But the flipside of this Alexander fixation, very much exemplified in Aurel Stein's career, is the extent to which pursuit of Alexander's legacy, by drawing archaeologists into central Asia, served to open up new, non-classical areas of research, and new insights into its history. DAFA's activities, in Bamiyan and elsewhere, also encouraged an official concern for archaeological remains. In Bamiyan moves were taken to consolidate and protect the archaeological site (families living in the caves were moved out, though refugees moved back in again during the civil wars: see Phil Grabsky's documentary, *The Boy Who Plays on the Buddhas of Bamiyan*; and the unstable niche of the smaller Buddha was given a massive concrete buttress), and the Buddhas started to feature in material representing the nation of Afghanistan – banknotes and stamps, for example – which began carrying images of the Buddhas in the 1930s.

The next generation of researchers in Bamiyan, in particular a flurry of activity in the 1970s (most notably Deborah Klimburg-Salter, Zemaryalai Tarzi and Takayasu Higuchi), concentrated on the wall paintings in the caves surrounding the Buddhas, and the consensus on the dating of the complex moved later: recent radiocarbon dating by German and Japanese teams of the Buddhas and the wall paintings has really only confirmed the essential conclusions reached by Tarzi and Klimburg-Salter (by comparative analysis of artistic styles) that the major development of the Buddhist community at Bamiyan dated from the sixth and seventh centuries AD. Higuchi and his team from Kyoto University made an invaluable contribution, particularly in view of subsequent events, in the shape of an exhaustive, four-volume inventory of the site, including a systematic description of surviving material and a detailed photographic database. It was the climax of a growing involvement in Bamiyan by Japanese archaeologists, for whom the place possessed as powerful a mystique as for Western visitors, but with an entirely different source in its status as an ancient site of Japan's national religion: 'This is a site, we could perhaps say,' explains Nobuko Inaba of the international NGO ICOMOS (International Council on Monuments and Sites), 'of dreams or of fantasy for Japanese people.' It is intriguing that Bamiyan could exert such a powerful allure simultaneously for both Europeans and Japanese, and intriguing also are attempts to ground that common interest in cultural history such as the joint Japan–Greece sponsored exhibition *Alexander the Great: East–West Cultural Contacts from Greece to Japan* staged in Japan in 2003, where (for example) the career of the Greek hero Heracles could be traced as he passed through central Asia and became

Vajrapani, companion of the Buddha, and thence on with Buddhism as far as Japan. The Japanese have taken a leading role in the excavation and preservation of Bamiyan since the destruction of 2001.

Zemaryalai Tarzi is a native Afghan, and in addition to his other research, he cooperated with a team from the Archaeological Survey of India, led by Rakhaldas Sengupta, which undertook a programme of consolidation of the Buddhas in the 1970s. Tarzi had to flee the brutal communist regime which preceded the Soviet intervention in 1979. Now a professor of archaeology at Strasbourg University, he has returned to Bamiyan since 2001, with French funding, as we saw in connection with the Great Stupa. But in 1979 the burgeoning archaeological activity across Afghanistan, which by that time was being pursued by many more nationalities than the French, came to an abrupt halt. Afghanistan being the archaeological treasure trove it is, remarkable things continued to come to light during the violent years that followed (the Bactrian documents from Rob, for example, one of which we heard from in Chapter 3, and a hoard of about 550,000 gold, silver and bronze coins and other precious objects from Mir Zakah, in eastern Afghanistan), and found their way directly onto the international art market.

What the 1960s and 70s had also brought to Bamiyan were increasing numbers of tourists, and the valley became an essential stop on the itineraries of the travel writers who proliferated in the later twentieth century, for whom the persistent mystique of Afghanistan exerted an irresistible appeal. Arnold J. Toynbee (1960), Freya Stark (1968), and Peter Levi and Bruce Chatwin (1970) all went to Bamiyan. For the less imaginative, their great forerunner, Robert Byron, seems to have set the tone of sceptical ambivalence towards the Buddhas: Stark talks of 'the huge and, let us face it, ugly Buddhas' who 'look out with absent minds, if any, and that rather lymphatic plumpness of Gandhara'; Peter Levi, more sympathetically, was put in mind of Robert Lowell's description of the image of Our Lady of Walsingham which 'expressionless, expresses God'. But what struck all of them was the peacefulness of the valley in which the Buddhas stood: Toynbee wrote of the 'peace in the glistening white poplartrunks ... peace in the shadowy shapes of the Buddhas and the caves', and Chatwin, who had travelled with Levi, and wrote the most powerful of these reminiscences (actually the introduction to a 1981 edition of Byron's *The Road to Oxiana*), excoriated the Soviet invaders of Afghanistan, ending with a lament for the sights, sounds, tastes and smells of the country, including memories of the Buddhas and Shahr-i Zohak – tokens of a peace that, he insisted, was now gone for ever. (I quoted part of his final paragraph at the head of Chapter 1.) We should not neglect in this connection Wilfred Thesiger, a refreshingly original kind of travel writer, who 'went to Afghanistan in the summer of 1954 from southern Iraq, where I had been for six months among the marshmen. There I had been living in semi-submerged houses and moving about in a canoe; now I was anxious to stretch my legs on the mountain tops.' Thesiger was in Afghanistan to study the Hazaras, but it was Hazaras in their pristine, traditional condition who interested him. His route through the highlands avoided – quite deliberately, one suspects – going anywhere near Bamiyan, which in Thesiger's view was no doubt a distraction from what was really important about the native people of the Hindu Kush. But Thesiger is very much the exception that proves the rule. For visitors to Afghanistan from the 1950s onwards, Bamiyan had retained its nineteenth-century status as the must-see location in the country.

THE ARCHAEOLOGISTS RETURN

When the archaeologists returned to Bamiyan after 2001, it was in obvious ways a demoralising sight. The Buddhas had, of course, been destroyed, but they were not the only victims of the recent troubles: whether by deliberate destruction, or looting for sale, it has been estimated that more than 80 per cent of the wall paintings recorded by the Kyoto expedition in the 1970s has also been lost. In a cave one visits on the way down from the top of the 38m Buddha niche, tyres were burned by the Taliban to blacken the ceiling and then white shoe prints (an Islamic insult) imprinted all over it; in another cave the tools that looters had been using to remove paintings for sale, no doubt exploiting the lack of security after the defeat of the Taliban, were found where they had hurriedly abandoned them. A measure taken almost immediately under efforts to safeguard what remained at Bamiyan (coordinated by UNESCO) was to close off caves with surviving paintings behind walls or locked doors, and to employ guards. But for all that, Bamiyan post-2001 was the focus of international attention to a degree it never had been before, and in archaeology that translates into funds. It is a paradox, but only superficially so, that some of the most exciting finds at Bamiyan, and most dramatic insights into the character of the Buddhist establishment there, have come in the decade since the destruction of the Buddhas.

In addition to evidence of the Great Stupa, Tarzi's

excavation of the 'Eastern Monastery' has yielded images of a courtyard around a small stupa, its walls lined with the feet and *samghati* hems of large clay statues of the Buddha, displaying a Greek style of drapery and in some cases retaining the original bold colours – a glimpse of the earlier history of Buddhist Bamiyan, before the construction of the Buddhas, a period when the dominant influence on Buddhist sculpture in this region was from Greco-Roman art, resulting in the remarkable artistic fusion known as Gandharan Art. Meanwhile researchers from the Technische Universität München, in a project under the aegis of ICOMOS, have studied how the Buddhas were constructed and decorated, and their conclusions underlay much of what I wrote on that topic in my first two chapters. One line of research which received considerable publicity was the radiocarbon dating of organic material retrieved from the debris of the Buddhas, which allowed the statues to be dated with some precision, and similar results have been achieved with the wall paintings, complicating in interesting ways our view of how and when and to what extent Bamiyan could be said to have embraced Islam: the research established that Buddhist art had continued to be created, especially in the side valleys of Kakrak and Fuladi, for some time after other evidence suggested that Bamiyan had been converted to Islam. Much publicity was also given to the discovery by other researchers in 2008 that paints used in wall paintings at Bamiyan contained 'drying oils', and thus could be counted as oil painting long before this technology became prevalent in the West.

Rather more tangibly, from the rubble of the smaller Buddha there also emerged two votive offerings which presumably date back to the statue's consecration. One of them, recovered in 2008, was found in a surviving section of the statue, in a crevice at the far back of the hole which had held the beam supporting the Buddha's right arm – in effect the location of the Buddha's elbow joint. The relic has not been opened, but it is a 4 × 6 × 3.5 cm cloth sack, tied with a thread, sealed with a clay seal, and with a circular base apparently indicating the presence of a coin. Two years earlier Edmund Melzl, who as a young man had taken that photograph of the VW Beetle between the larger Buddha's feet, found another votive deposit in the debris between the smaller Buddha's feet, a textile pouch containing metal artefacts, pellets thought to contain ashes of the Buddha, and fragments of a leaf that turned out to be from a *Ficus religiosa* or Bodhi tree, the species under which the Buddha achieved enlightenment. The assumption must be that the leaf was from that very Bodhi tree at Bodh Gaya in Bihar, India. There were also fragments on birch bark of a very common Sanskrit text, a kind of Buddhist credo or condensation of all the Buddha's teachings, 'Those phenomena which arise from a cause,/ the Tathagata ['one who has attained what is really so'] declared what is their cause/ and what is their cessation./ Thus the great Mendicant has spoken.' This text was believed to have the power of a charm, presumably protecting the statue in which it was secreted. But the religious principle it expresses also has implications capable of rendering both the creation of this gigantic statue and its destruction 1,400 years later (and everything in between) events of singular unimportance.

Both these last relics were ceremoniously presented to Habiba Sarabi, the Governor of Bamiyan province, and the plan seems to be that in the fullness of time they will go to a proposed Museum of Bamiyan. Another recent find allegedly at Bamiyan poses issues of ownership more pointedly, and has become a cause célèbre for opponents of the international trade in antiquities. It is a cache of Buddhist manuscripts, written on palm leaf, birch bark, vellum and copper, apparently discovered in the mid-1990s (the middle of the civil war). They are the remains of what has been described as a library of up to 1,000 Buddhist manuscripts, or perhaps a kind of *genizah* or disposal of texts which had been superseded but were too sacred to destroy. Most of these texts have been acquired by the Norwegian collector Martin Schøyen and are now in Oslo. The story of their discovery and acquisition is in fact extremely murky, and there is a suspicion, voiced in a critical TV exposé on the public broadcaster NRK in Norway, that Bamiyan has been claimed as the find spot because of its instant association with threatened world heritage, an unanswerable example of historical material better off outside its country of origin. The Japanese archaeologist Kazuya Yamauchi believes that their source was a cave at Zargaran, a kilometre or so east of the main Buddha cliff. Critics argue that collectors like Schøyen encourage irresponsible excavations, as a consequence of which the crucial explanatory context of archaeological discoveries is lost, and local or national communities lose artefacts that are rightly theirs. Schøyen has responded to the last point, rejecting any call to repatriate the manuscripts, on two main grounds – that security in Afghanistan is inadequate at the moment, which is reasonable enough, and then a rather muddily argued claim to the effect that Afghanistan is in a deeper sense a place intolerant of Buddhist remains: 'More tragically, the Buddhist monasteries and their manuscripts were mostly destroyed in the eighth century by Muslim invaders.

The remaining sites were, to a greater extent, destroyed by the Taliban very recently, including, most infamously, the two giant statues of the Buddha that were blown up in 2001' (from the Schøyen Collection website). The acquisition of the manuscripts is presented as a rescue mission for the 'common heritage of mankind', enshrined in a process of publication of the manuscripts which will make them available to everyone.

Principle and practicality seem hopelessly confused here. In the particular circumstances of Taliban-controlled Afghanistan, we may be thankful that material was not available to be destroyed, although we must not allow ourselves to accept the implication that the Taliban attitude to Buddhist artefacts is representative of Islamic attitudes in general: as we know, 'Buddhist monasteries and their manuscripts' were *not* destroyed by the 'Muslim invaders', who were in fact strikingly tolerant of other faiths. But it seems self-evident to me that archaeological material should be where it can do most good, and that if (and that is undoubtedly a big 'if') security can be properly established in Afghanistan, the manuscripts should return to Bamiyan, always assuming that it was indeed from there or thereabouts that they originated. The value of a Bamiyan Museum which could display such items for civic pride and cohesion, for education of the young, and for tourism (within Afghanistan, and one day even beyond), would be immeasurable. But I should backtrack a little here. Why should they be returned to a Bamiyan Museum, and not the National Museum of Afghanistan in Kabul? The importance of a regional museum will best be explained by returning to Abdur Rahman and starting our historical progression again, but this time talking not about the antiquities of Bamiyan, but about its people.

As we have repeatedly seen in passing – and as is anyway familiar to readers of Khaled Hosseini's bestseller *The Kite Runner* – the Hazara people of the north-central highlands of Afghanistan have been the targets of intense discrimination in modern Afghanistan. This has a lot to do with religious differences: the vast majority of Hazaras follow the Shi'ite branch of Islam, while the rest of Afghanistan is almost exclusively Sunni. But serious difficulties for the Hazaras date to the late nineteenth century and the rule of Abdur Rahman, the talented but ruthless 'Iron Amir' of Afghanistan in the last two decades of the nineteenth century who undertook an ambitious, and often brutal, series of campaigns to unify Afghanistan, aided by generous subsidies from the British (offered in return for control of Afghanistan's foreign affairs, the arrangement that lasted until 1919). Abdur Rahman was an authentic product of the brutal dynastic politics of the Afghan royal family, which had seen him fight repeated wars against relatives, and spend a long period in exile, before securing the throne; he was clever and decisive, but still essentially medieval in his methodology, a man who, while obviously taking lessons from Bismarck's Germany, also once had a man's lips sewn shut when he dared to discuss politics. Abdur Rahman's aim was to turn the diverse population of Afghanistan, a product in equal measure of the geography of the country and its complex history, into a modern nation-state. In the case of the Hazarajat, the ancestral homeland of the Hazaras, this meant measures to incorporate a formerly autonomous territory and people into a state under the firm rule of Kabul. The result was predictably violent: resistance from Hazaras when Kabul didn't follow its traditional policy of taxing them and

27. Abdur Rahman, Amir of Afghanistan from 1880 to 1901, in a painting by his one-time surgeon, J. A. Gray. Abdur Rahman was the most influential of the modern rulers of Afghanistan, a moderniser with a ruthless streak, and much of the character of present-day Afghanistan can be traced to his reign.

then leaving them alone; and massacres, forced relocations and enslavement by Abdur Rahman's forces as they enforced Kabul's permanent control. Traditional Hazara society was shattered, and displaced Hazara communities appeared in the cities of Afghanistan, especially Kabul and Mazar-i Sharif, very much in the role of an impoverished and disenfranchised underclass: Hazaras typically worked as servants; the saying *Hazara wa chaklet*, 'Hazara and chocolate', meant 'Too big for his boots'. Hazaras also went abroad, to Iran or British India: it was Hazaras in modern Pakistan, the descendants of exiles or refugees from the period of Abdur Rahman, who provided DNA samples for the genetic research mentioned in Chapter 3. Another legacy of this migration was a regiment called the 10th Hazara Pioneers fighting on the Western Front in 1915 ('probably the best shooting regiment in the Indian Army,' according to Wilfred Thesiger).

Discrimination against Hazaras was officially enforced: Shi'i law was not recognised, and Shi'i religious practices such as the commemoration of the death of Hussain, grandson of the Prophet, at Ashura, were banned. Hazaras enjoyed very little social mobility, being systematically excluded from educational opportunities and from jobs in the public service or the upper echelons of the military. Such economic advances as there were in Afghanistan during the twentieth century, for example the construction of a so-called national 'Ring Road' linking the main cities, and the Salang Tunnel, which provided a more direct route through the Hindu Kush between Kabul and the north of the country, only served to isolate further the mountain communities, and no attempt was made to broaden the transport infrastructure so as to link these main routes with the hinterland. In general Abdur Rahman's policy of unification, which was maintained by his successors, lacked any coherent economic dimension. No thought was given to encouraging the economic conditions which might have knitted the various communities of Afghanistan together much more effectively and lastingly than Abdur Rahman's preferred strategy of armed force. The effects of this malign neglect were particularly felt in the early 1970s, when a drought caused famine which was especially acute in areas, the Hazarajat above all, which had been left isolated by Afghanistan's inadequate transport system.

In political terms, the Afghan state that Abdur Rahman and his successors set out to create was one dominated by the largest ethnic group, the Pashtuns. The Hazaras especially had little or no stake in this conception of the nation of Afghanistan. The enormities committed against the Hazara people by the Taliban, who were simultaneously an essentially Pashtun organisation and a radically Sunni one, marked an extreme expression of this prejudice against the Hazaras: in Mazar-i Sharif in 1998 at least two thousand civilians, predominantly Hazaras, were systematically slaughtered by Taliban forces, and while there was horror perpetrated by all sides in the Afghan civil war, that ghastly event reflected more than any the deep-seated Pashtun chauvinism of the Taliban. In Bamiyan itself Taliban conquest became very readily a raw question of *Lebensraum*. Another legacy of Abdur Rahman was perennial conflict over land use between sedentary Hazara farmers and the predominantly Pashtun Kuchi nomads. Taliban activity in Bamiyan often seemed to be an attempt to resolve that conflict once and for all in favour of Pashtuns, an effective ethnic cleansing. At Fuladi in 1999 locals were told, 'You should leave. The land does not belong to you': the menfolk were arrested, and in many cases shot, houses and at least one mosque were burned, and livestock was looted. After the fall of the Taliban in 2001 it was found that a Kuchi cemetery near Bamiyan, known locally as the Qabr-i Afghan, the Afghan Cemetery (an indication of how closely identified the very notions of 'Afghan' and 'Pashtun' have been), was found vandalised.

But the Hazara people have displayed a remarkable resilience, much in evidence since 2001. Despite their history, recent and not so recent, they have emerged, in many ways, the most dynamic of the ethnic components of today's Afghanistan: a disciplined political force, a remarkably conciliatory presence (in the circumstances) in national politics, and a community passionately committed to education. A number of factors have contributed to their renewed confidence. Some of it may even date back to the Soviet occupation, when a generally misconceived imposition of Marxist doctrine on a country that lacked an industrial working class at any rate brought some benefit to the underprivileged Hazaras: a token of the change to their status was that from 1981–8 and 1989–90 the prime minister of Afghanistan (a less powerful position than it sounds, admittedly) was a Hazara, Sultan Ali Keshtmand. (He now lives in London, and, the way things are, his tenure as prime minister was regarded by some non-Hazara mujahedin as an additional reason to resist the Communist government.) Also relevant are longer historical processes, the growth of a Hazara middle class in the cities, which is an unforeseen consequence of Abdur Rahman's repressive measures, since the social system in the Hazarajat which he effectively destroyed had been a rigidly feudal one. And we cannot ignore the impact of the refugee experience: Hazaras who left Afghanistan in the chaos of the eighties or nineties mainly went to Iran, where their children, male and female, enjoyed free education and were also potentially exposed to the comparatively modern and sophisticated youth culture of that country.

Whatever the causes, the result is an unusually self-aware and politicised community, with literacy rates well above the national average and, because of their pragmatic approach to politics, a disproportionate influence at a national level. (Hazaras are reckoned to constitute somewhere between 9 and 13 per cent of the population.) We should not overstate this: Timor Sharan, a British Hazara working in Kabul, vividly described to me how, every morning, he would see a tide of Hazaras heading for the centre of the city – who were subsequently entirely invisible whenever he visited central Kabul: Hazaras in the cities are still typically employed in menial work. The Hazarajat itself is poor and backward, even by Afghan standards, and while, according to Olivier Roy (writing in 1985), 'the educated Shi'a are very conscious of their position as a minority and are noted for political activism', the Hazara peasantry remain 'untouched by the modern world'. But the 2004 constitution recognised Shi'i law, a university has functioned in Bamiyan since 1996, and Hazaras do now for the first time have a tangible stake in their country. An especially powerful moment in Havana Marking's superb documentary about *Afghan Star*, the Afghan version of *Pop Idol* (also the name of Marking's film, which is certainly the best introduction to contemporary Afghanistan), is when the Hazara finalist, Hamid Sakhizada, sings the composition of another Hazara, Safdar Tawakoli, which begins, 'Whether we are from Bamiyan or Qandahar, we are all one brother …', a Hazara celebrating national unity (Qandahar being in the Pashtun heartland) with a moral authority only Hazaras can claim. Bamiyan itself has developed a lively civil society, notable for punchy and good-humoured demonstrations against central government's shortcomings (for example, a march culminating in the erection of a giant oil lamp at a roundabout in May 2011, to protest the delay in introducing public electricity), which should make it a model for the rest of the country. The economic prospects of the Hazarajat may also shortly be transformed, when a huge deposit of iron ore at Hajigak south of Bamiyan (described as the largest remaining in Asia) begins to be exploited, a development which of course carries risks as immense as the opportunities; there is persistent talk of a railway link to the north and/or to the east to join up with the copper mine at Mes Ainak. I myself have seen some dramatic improvements (albeit still very patchy) to Bamiyan's road communications: a journey from Bamiyan to the National Park at Band-i Amir took half as long in 2011 as it had in 2009. Similarly cautious approval could be given of Bamiyan town itself, now boasting a population of 73,000, yet still lacking that publicly generated electricity. At present this is still an almost exclusively agricultural economy, very dependent on the potato crop (for which Bamiyan is renowned). There is potential, but it is fragile.

A MUSEUM FOR BAMIYAN

How does the archaeology of Bamiyan fit into all this? One way into that question is to recognise that Abdur Rahman's quest for a strong, unified nation-state was an anomalous project in the long history of Afghanistan. What happened during the Soviet occupation and the civil wars that followed, as the various regions of Afghanistan established effectively independent jurisdictions, was really just a re-emergence of the old functional system of regional autonomy that has been the norm in this region since at least Puluo in the eighth century, and no doubt long before him. Afghanistan is too disparate, geographically and culturally, ever to be a conventional nation-state, and a sensible approach to stabilising the country would acknowledge that over-centralised models of government (such as the one in place since 2001) will never make sense of what a Soviet general called 'the fundamental characteristic of Afghan society – its incoherence', the fundamentally atomised nature of Afghanistan, in which local loyalties always trump national. Abdur Rahman and his successors sought to construct a strong Afghan state, and it was a strongly Pashtun state, too. Abdur Rahman's grandson, Amanullah, while liberal in certain respects, did not diverge either from the nationalism of his predecessors or the Pashtun bias of their administrations. Thus when he established the National Museum of Afghanistan and entered the arrangement with Albert Foucher which created DAFA, one cannot in all conscience divorce his cultural policy, in many ways so enlightened, from his state-building. The stirring motto of the National Museum has been much bandied about in connection with the looting and destruction of Afghan antiquities in the civil war and Taliban period: 'A nation stays alive when its culture stays alive.' But the formulation, it must be said, is snappier in English than in Persian, and begs a cartload of questions (What nation? Whose nation? Whose culture?); it is also fatally tainted by the atmosphere of non-inclusive nationalism in which the National Museum was conceived.

Amanullah's adviser and father-in-law, Mahmud Tarzi, one of Afghanistan's greatest intellectual figures, used very similar terms to convey the importance of what he called 'our national language Pashtu', the language of the Pashtuns spoken by a minority of the people of Afghanistan: 'A nation which loses its language also loses its life.' That would be a national language, and indeed a concept of nationhood, unintelligible to most of the Persian-speaking population of Bamiyan, for a start.

Afghanistan needs (and is experiencing, willy-nilly) a rebalancing of its power structure, albeit in conditions that could hardly be less congenial for the kind of generous compromises ideally required. But if Pashtuns will have to accept that their right to rule is not God-given, and Afghans in general that Hazaras have as much right to a voice and influence as any other group, Kabul (and any government based there) will also need to get used once again to powerful and assertive regions possessing significant autonomy. That will inevitably find a reflection in cultural policy. If Bamiyan has a university, it should also have a museum, and a presumptive claim on archaeological finds made there. The National Museum remains essential – one of the very striking things about contemporary Afghanistan is the lack of any significant pressure to break up this troubled and divided country (Barfield talks of 'a united people in a failed state') – but it will, like the nation it embodies, only be strengthened by partnership with a network of museums throughout the country.

All this talk of cultural policies is, of course, moonshine until security is permanently established, and no one knows when that will be. But let us indulge the fantasy a little longer. What the people of Bamiyan hope for more than anything else is a return of the tourist industry that existed in the 1960s and 70s: when foreign visitors stayed in a hotel of yurts (still possible, if it's to your taste, at the Roof of Bamyan Hotel), and took a day trip to the sapphire-blue lakes at Band-i Amir. I have been amazed how many people in their fifties or sixties I've encountered while researching this book who visited Bamiyan at that time: there is a huge, untapped resource of private photographs, all of them terribly evocative for someone who has seen only the empty niches. Today sterling efforts are being made to encourage the tourists back again. Well-presented pamphlets describe the various historical sites, and there are new brass plaques at each, with descriptions in Persian and English. The emphasis is on a 'sustainable' tourism, the benefits of which will find their way quickly to the local people. The target market is potentially diverse: visitors interested in wildlife, battlefields or simply stunning natural beauty are going to find as much to appeal to them here as those with a specific interest in the archaeological remains. But tourists in significant numbers will only come when access, by road or air, is improved (it is still an uncomfortable trip from Kabul by road for most of the distance, and air access at present is generally only for aid and development workers and UN employees), and when there is security. Bamiyan province itself is currently the safest place in Afghanistan, and a sign of this was that it was the first area of the country to be transferred to Afghan security control from ISAF in 2011. The access routes between Kabul and Bamiyan are currently another matter.

A lot of these issues converge in debates about the possible reconstruction of the Buddhas, for which, it is fair to say, there is much support in Bamiyan (very much with an eye on potential tourism) and considerable resistance in the international academic community. Proposals to recreate the Buddhas in concrete or resin, or in the form of a laser light-show, have been felt to transgress certain fundamental archaeological principles, as well as risking serious opposition in a country of deep religious conservatism which, while it might not approve of the *destruction* of Buddha statues, could nevertheless find the (re)construction of such images hard to stomach. To most they also seem in fundamentally poor taste. On the contrary, the empty niches have seemed to many a powerful monument in their own right. This point has been most articulately made by Ikuo Hirayama, whose epiphany before the Buddha cliff we read about at the start of Chapter 2, and who in 2002 pleaded that the site be left as it is, and any money raised for reconstruction be spent on humanitarian relief of refugees instead. 'There are other world cultural heritages that memorialise atrocities,' he insisted, citing Auschwitz and the Atomic Bomb Dome in Hiroshima: 'I suggest that the Bamiyan caves be preserved as a symbolic reminder of the barbaric destruction of culture by human beings.' The only kind of reconstruction acceptable to the archaeological establishment is the process known as 'anastylosis', the recomposition of a collapsed monument using its surviving fragments with only the very minimum of foreign materials, and those that there are clearly differentiated as such. The leading champion of anastylosis at Bamiyan is Michael Petzet, former President of ICOMOS, the historical conservation NGO, and, always assuming there are enough fragments for anastylosis to proceed, the project does seem an admirable marriage of exemplary archaeological practice and the real interests of the local community, a compromise (in other words) between the claims of mankind and those of the people of Bamiyan, and Afghanistan. That said, the cost of the process would be exorbitant, the expenditure justifiable only if a proportionate benefit to the people of Bamiyan were assured. Perhaps the Indian and Canadian firms that have won the contract to extract iron from Hajigak might act as corporate sponsors ...

LA PAISIBLE VALLÉE

Such thoughts are strictly academic unless the peace that has reigned in Bamiyan for the last decade is allowed to persist. Much heartfelt effort has been put into compensating for the terrible events that happened here, and I am referring to the immense human suffering ahead of the comparatively insignificant damage to inanimate monuments. A culture of blame and condemnation has developed around foreign involvement in Afghanistan, but I confess that all I have witnessed is well-meaning people wrestling with an intractable problem, a country where both too much and too little intervention seem equally culpable. But the wider world has undoubtedly brought benefit to Bamiyan in recent years, and it might be exemplified by the work of the ATC demining agency which, under the aegis of the (strictly non-aligned) UN agency MACCA (Mine Action Coordination Centre for Afghanistan), and in cooperation with UNESCO, has cleared mines and unexploded ordnance from the Buddha niches, Shahr-i Zohak, Shahr-i Gholghola and other archaeological sites around Bamiyan, employing special procedures to avoid damage to archaeological material. (An archaeologist commented how good the mine clearers were at excavating archaeological artefacts: the care and delicacy they had learned in mine clearance was the perfect transferable skill.) Before they thought about clearing the historical sites, needless to say, they cleared the inhabited areas and farmland. I am biased, because it was the kindness of mine clearers that allowed me to visit this beautiful place, but the removal of explosive material from the everyday environment of working farmers or playing children or indeed archaeologists seeking to understand how the Buddhas were constructed and even how they might be constructed anew – I cannot think of any activity more uncontroversially praiseworthy.

The bigger scene is not too encouraging at present. Shortly after my last visit, in June 2011, the popular (elected) chairman of the Bamiyan Provincial Council, Jawad Zohak, was murdered as he travelled by car to Kabul through the Ghurband valley in Parwan province, east of Bamiyan: by all accounts, if anyone embodied the best potential of Bamiyan's burgeoning civil society, it was he. There are clear attempts to undermine security in Bamiyan: my hosts in May 2011 were nervous when I wanted to visit areas close to the border with Baghlan province to the north-east – the first and thus far only casualty suffered by the New Zealand ISAF forces with responsibility for Bamiyan province happened close to that border in August 2010. The potential for ethnic/sectarian violence to reignite is significant, and recent bomb attacks directed at the Shiʻa of Kabul and Mazar-i Sharif are designed to drive communities apart. I hardly need to say what a catastrophe it would be if all that has been achieved in Bamiyan (for all that it is never as much as might have been) were reversed.

Peace, pure and simple, is worth a hundred development projects, of course, and peace, despite everything, seems to

28. A deminer from the ATC demining agency at work on the site of Shahr-i Zohak. It is a massive task to clear the mines and unexploded ordnance that are the legacy of decades of conflict in Afghanistan, but remarkable progress has been made. In the three months to September 2011, 67 Afghans were killed or injured by mines, over 80 per cent of whom were children; the monthly average of casualties a decade ago was 176. In the same time period 7,793 anti-personnel mines, 265 anti-tank mines, 45 abandoned improvised explosive devices and 182,663 explosive remnants of war were destroyed.

me, as it has to many others, the characteristic condition of Bamiyan. It was a representative of MACCA in Bamiyan, Mehrab Shah Afzali from Kabul, who, in conversation with me, once searched for the right English word to describe his overriding impression of the Bamiyan valley and its people. It was, he said, the 'calmest' place he had ever been. He was translating the Persian superlative *ārāmtarīn*, *ārām* being (like 'calm') both an adjective, 'peaceful', 'tranquil', and a noun, 'tranquillity', 'peace'. Sultan Muhammad's fellow travellers in 1528 *ārām gereftand*, 'found peace', under the niche of the 38m Buddha, and it was the peculiar *ārām* of the Bamiyan valley, I think, that affected Lieutenant Vincent Eyre as he sat on the head of that Buddha and gazed at the view, forgetting for an instant the awful prospect of slavery facing him, his wife, and his young son. It was certainly as a study in pastoral tranquillity that Lieutenant John Sturt sketched the valley below Shahr-i Zohak. '*La paisible vallée*' is Zemaryalai Tarzi's favoured way of referring to Bamiyan, and it is a particularly profound concept of peace that is represented by the figure, discovered by Tarzi's team, of the reclining, smiling Buddha at the point of attaining ultimate nirvana, the deeper release promised to the exhausted merchants or pilgrims resting at the green oasis of Bamiyan following their arduous crossing of the mountains. To that I can add only that it was in this beautiful valley, which has been a wonder for adherents of at least three world religions, that a Church of England-raised atheist, the author, experienced a moment of intense peace, gazing at night across the Valley of Bamiyan to the Buddha cliffs, while the muezzin at the town mosque sang the Call to Prayer.

FURTHER READING

GENERAL

An essential first step to understanding any particular part of Afghanistan, or specific period of its history, is to get a broader sense of its history and complex ethnic composition, themselves in turn largely shaped by the country's dramatic geographical character. A readable, comprehensive and up-to-date account of Afghanistan is T. Barfield, *Afghanistan: A Cultural and Political History* (Princeton, 2010); while W. Vogelsang, *The Afghans* (Chichester, 2002) offers a blow-by-blow account of the country's complex history from its beginnings. A staple of every ex-pat's bookshelf is L. Dupree, *Afghanistan*, 2nd edn (Karachi and Oxford, 1997), an idiosyn-cratic but exceptionally well-informed account of the geog-raphy, history, ethnography and folk culture of the country. For the archaeology of Afghanistan, W. Ball, *The Monuments of Afghanistan* (New York and London, 2008) is a richly illus-trated account by a leading authority; and the shorter work of E. Knobloch, *The Archaeology and Architecture of Afghanistan* (Stroud, 2002) is also very informative: both also provide excel-lent explanations of the historical and geographical context of the archaeology. B. Omrani and M. Leeming, *Afghanistan: A Companion and Guide* (Leicester, 2004) combines sumptuous colour images of Afghanistan from before the Soviet invasion with the accounts of earlier visitors to produce a seductive portrait of the country; Havana Marking's film documentary *Afghan Star* (2009) and A. Loewen and J. McMichael, *Images of Afghanistan* (Oxford, 2010) convey contemporary Afghanistan more realistically. P. Docherty, *The Khyber Pass* (London, 2007) is an extremely enjoyable history of another 'Gate to India'.

BAMIYAN: SITE AND ARCHAEOLOGY

There is a succinct description and history of the valley of Bamiyan in the *Encyclopedia of Islam*, 2nd edn, vol. I, 1009. Alfred Foucher's account of Bamiyan came in a letter to the President of the Société Asiatique in *Journal Asiatique* 202 (1923), 354–68; and N. H. Dupree's tourist guides from the 1960s and 70s, *The Valley of Bamiyan*, 2nd edn (Kabul, 1967), and *An Historical Guide to Afghanistan*, 2nd edn (Kabul, 1977) are still informative. Detailed archaeological and art historical descriptions of the Buddhas, caves, and other antiquities include publications by the Délégation archéologique française en Afghanistan (DAFA): A. and Y. Godard and J. Hackin, *Les antiquités bouddhiques de Bamiyan* (Paris, 1928), and J. Hackin and J. Carl, *Nouvelles recherches archéologiques à Bamiyan* (Paris, 1933). See also Z. Tarzi, *L'architecture et le décor rupestre des grottes de Bamiyan* (Paris, 1977), and D. Klimburg-Salter, *The Kingdom of Bamiyan* (Naples, 1989). A speculative, but interesting, theory on the identity of the figure in the horse-drawn chariot in the soffit of the smaller niche is F. Grenet, 'Bamiyan and the *Mir Yasht*', *Bulletin of the Asia Institute* 7 (1993–4), 87–94. The monumental four-volume Kyoto publication, T. Higuchi (ed.), *Bamiyan* (Kyoto, 1984) is in Japanese, but since 2001 a series of bilingual publications concerned with preserving what survives at Bamiyan, and further archaeological investigation, have been published by the Japan Centre for International Cooperation in Conservation: for example, *Preserving Bamiyan* (Tokyo, 2005), which describes among other things the emergency measures taken after the fall of the Taliban, and also includes discussion of the possible reconstruction of the Buddhas; and *Radiocarbon Dating of the Bamiyan Mural Paintings* (Tokyo, 2006). There is interesting material also in two French publications, *L'art d'Afghanistan* (Paris, 2007), and *Paysages du centre de l'Afghanistan* (Paris, 2010). Tarzi has described his recent discoveries at Bamiyan in various Japanese and French publications, but his most comprehensive account is 'Bamiyan (Afghanistan): Récentes fouilles françaises (2002–2006)', *Comptes rendus des séances de l'Académie des Inscriptions et Belles-lettres* (CRAI) 2007, 877–925. The ICOMOS publication M. Petzet (ed.), *The Giant Buddhas of Bamiyan: Safeguarding the Remains* (Berlin, 2009) describes in marvellous detail the research undertaken on the fragments of the Buddhas.

The most detailed investigation of Shahr-i Zohak is P. H. B. Baker and F. R. Allchin, *Shahr-i Zohak and the History of the Bamiyan Valley, Afghanistan* (Oxford, 1991), and a broader perspective on the archaeology of the region is provided by another DAFA publication, M. Le Berre, *Monuments pré-islamiques de l'Hindukush central* (Paris, 1987).

THE DESTRUCTION

Images of the destruction of the Buddhas in 2001 are shown

in C. Frei's film *The Giant Buddhas* (2005), which also features interviews with Taisir Alluni and Zemaryalai Tarzi. T. Barfield, 'Idol threats', *Religion in the News* 4.2 (2001) is a more-or-less instantaneous reaction from a well-informed observer. What was happening within the leadership of the Taliban, and the growing influence of bin Laden, has been clarified since by R. Gutman, *How We Missed the Story* (Washington, DC, 2008). The rise, fall, and resurgence of the Taliban has been chronicled by Ahmed Rashid in various editions of *Taliban* and more recently *Descent into Chaos* (London, 2008), and by J. Fergusson, *Taliban* (London, 2010); and the development and character of Al-Qa'ida in L. Wright, *The Looming Tower* (London, 2006) and J. Burke, *Al-Qaeda*, 3rd edn (London, 2007). Olivier Roy's penetrating analysis of Al-Qa'ida after bin Laden's death was in the *New Statesman*, 12 May 2011. The 'Abrahamic' imagery of the destruction of the Buddhas is explained in J. J. Elias, '(Un)making idolatry: From Mecca to Bamiyan', *Future Anterior* 4.2 (2007), 12–29; and A. J. Silverstein, *Islamic History: A Very Short Introduction* (Oxford, 2010) is an excellent preliminary account of traditional Islamic modes of thought. D. Gillman, *The Idea of Cultural Heritage*, rev. edn (Cambridge, 2010) explains how that notion has developed.

THE BUDDHIST CENTURIES

A good way into the decidedly complex religion of Buddhism is D. Keown, *Buddhism: A Very Short Introduction* (Oxford, 1996). A rather bigger book, but an excellent introduction to Buddhism as well as a very beautiful thing, is D. L. Snellgrove (ed.), *The Image of the Buddha* (London and Paris, 1978), which traces the dramatic changes, as well as the continuities, in the representation of the Buddha over time and in the different regions of Asia where Buddhism prevailed. Those of bolder disposition may be prepared to tackle an account of the numerous sects of Hinayana Buddhism: A. Bareau, *Les sectes bouddhiques du Petit Véhicule* (Saigon, 1955). D. Seckel, *The Art of Buddhism* (London, 1964) explains with impressive clarity the characteristic architectural forms of Buddhism, as well as the artistic. The most important contribution to the history of Buddhist Bamiyan is S. Kuwayama, 'Two itineraries concerning the emergence of the colossi at Bamiyan', in G. Gnoli and L. Lanciotti, *Orientalia Iosephi Tucci memoriae dicata* (Rome, 1985–8), 703–27, which established the mid-sixth century as a critical turning-point. For the historical context see also D. Klimburg-Salter, 'Buddhist painting in the Hindu Kush ca. VIIth to Xth centuries', in É. de la Vaissière, *Islamisation de l'Asie centrale* (Paris, 2008), 131–59, and also her article in *Paysages du centre de l'Afghanistan* (Paris, 2010), 173–92. Klimburg-Salter's 'Bamiyan: An obituary and a glance towards the future', *Oriental Art* 49 (2003), 2–12 is an encapsulation of the current understanding of the Bamiyan site aimed at the more general reader. B. A. Litvinsky (ed.), *History of the Civilizations of Central Asia*, vol. III (Paris, 1996) offers a broad account of developments in the region from AD 250 to 750; and A. Wink, *Al-Hind: The Making of the Indo-Islamic World*, vol. I (1990), 109–92 details the religions and cultures encountered by Muslim forces at their eastern frontier. For the earlier history of Buddhism in Afghanistan and its vicinity see E. Errington and J. Cribb, *The Crossroads of Asia* (Cambridge, 1992).

The letter of Puluo to the emperor of China is translated

into French by E. Chavannes, *Documents sur les Tou-kiue (Turcs) Occidentaux* (St Petersburg, 1903), 200–202. Huili's life of Xuanzang and Xuanzang's dictated account were translated by S. Beal as *The Life of Hiuen Tsiang by the Shaman Hwui Li* (London, 1888) and *Si-Yu-Ki: Buddhist Records of the Western World* (London, 1906); a recent translation of the latter text is L. Rongxi, *The Great Tang Dynasty Record of the Western Regions* (Berkeley, 1996), and S. H. Wriggins, *The Silk Road Journey with Xuanzang* (Boulder, 2004) is a very readable account of the pilgrim's life and achievement. Hyecho's narrative of his travels in the following century, discovered as recently as 1908, is translated and annotated by H.-S. Yang, Y.-H. Jan, S. Iida and L. W. Preston, *The Hye Ch'o Diary* (Berkeley, 1984). DAFA's discoveries at the monastery site of Fondukistan in the Ghurband valley are well encapsulated by S. Novotny, 'The Buddhist Monastery of Fondukistan, Afghanistan: A reconstruction', *Journal of Inner Asian Art and Archaeology* 2 (2007), 31–7. For the broader context of the Buddhist world at the time, see F. Wood, *The Silk Road* (London, 2003), chap. 7; the rest of the book is a fascinating account of East–West communication through central Asia from the beginnings to the present day. A vivid insight into eighth-century Buddhist culture (and indeed twenty-first-century Afghan politics) is provided by J. Lee and N. Sims-Williams, 'The antiquities and inscription of Tang-i Safedak', *Silk Road Art and Archaeology* 9 (2003), 159–84.

THE ISLAMIC CENTURIES

An extremely useful general source of information is the online *Encyclopedia Iranica* (www.iranicaonline.org/). Babur's memoirs are translated by W. M. Thackston, *The Baburnama* (Washington, DC, 1996), and Ghaffar Khan's autobiography was published as *My Life and Struggle* (Delhi, 1969). F. B. Flood, 'Between cult and culture: Bamiyan, Islamic iconoclasm, and the museum', *The Art Bulletin* 84 (2002), 641–59, is a brilliant discussion of Islamic attitudes to figurative art in the light of the destruction of the Buddhas of Bamiyan, itself indebted to A. S. Melikian-Chirvani, 'L'évocation littéraire du bouddhisme dans l'Iran musulman', *Le Monde Iranien et l'Islam* 2 (Geneva, 1974), 1–72, an exceptionally rich account of the continuities between the pre-Islamic and Islamic cultures of medieval Iran. The observation that Ghaznavid mural painting at Lashkari Bazar owes a lot to pre-Islamic traditions is made by O. Grabar, *Mostly Miniatures* (Princeton, 2000), 37. The *Fihrist of Al-Nadim* was translated into English by B. Dodge (New York, 1970), and the historical context of the Barmakids can be followed up in H. Kennedy, *The Prophet and the Age of the Caliphates* (New York, 1986) and *The Court of the Caliphs* (London, 2004), which was published in the USA as *When Baghdad Ruled the Muslim World* (Cambridge, MA, 2005): the connection between 'Barmak' and 'pramukha' was seen by H. W. Bailey, 'Iranica', *Bulletin of the School of Oriental and African Studies* 11 (1943), 1–5. For the Islamic conquest of Afghanistan see E. Bosworth, 'The Appearance and Establishment of Islam in Afghanistan', in É. de la Vaissière, *Islamisation de l'Asie centrale* (Paris, 2008), 97–114.

The era of Al-Biruni and Onsori is well described in E. Bosworth, *The Ghaznavids* (Edinburgh, 1963). References to Bamiyan in Islamic sources are collected by G. Le Strange, *The Lands of the Eastern Caliphate* (Cambridge, 1905), 418–19, although this is less than 100 per cent accurate. The eleventh-century prenuptial agreement from Bamiyan has been discussed in a series of articles by G. Scarcia, including 'A preliminary report on a Persian legal document of 470–1078 found at Bamiyan', *East & West* 14 (1963), 73–85, and 'An edition of the Persian legal document from Bamiyan', *East & West* 16 (1966), 290–95: in the first Scarcia also provides a very useful summary history of Bamiyan from the ninth to the eleventh century. The documents from the eve of the Mongol invasion in the thirteenth century are described in V. Minorsky, 'Some early documents in Persian (II)', *Journal of the Royal Asiatic Society of Great Britain and Ireland* 1 (1943), 86–99: another way into the Ghurid period is the DAFA account of the Ghurid capital at Firuzkuh, A. Maricq and G. Wiet, *Le minaret de Djam* (Paris, 1959). The Bactrian texts from the archive of Rob are published, with a translation, by N. Sims-Williams, *Bactrian Documents from Northern Afghanistan*, Part 1 (Oxford, 2000), and Sims-Williams introduces the material in a published lecture, *Recent Discoveries in the Bactrian Language and their Historical Significance* (Kabul, 2004), which is also available online: www.gengo.1.u-tokyo. ac.jp/~hkum/bactrian.html. D. N. Maclean, *Religion and Society in Arab Sind* (Leiden, 1989) is a brilliant analysis of the process of conversion to Islam. For my reading of Tusi's *'Aja'ib al-makhluqat* I am indebted to O. Pancaroğlou, 'Signs in the horizons: Concepts of image and boundary in a medieval Persian cosmography', *RES: Anthropology and Aesthetics* 43 (2003), 31–41. Juvaini's history of Genghis Khan has been translated by J. A. Boyle (Manchester, 1997), and in T. Mackintosh-Smith, *The Travels of Ibn Battutah* (London, 2002), there is an abridged translation of the memoirs of the greatest of all travellers. The Packard Humanities Institute hosts a translation of the *A'in-i Akbari* on its Persian Literature in Translation website (http://persian.packhum.org/persian/), but Sultan Muhammad's *Majma' al-ghara'ib* exists only in manuscript: the quoted text was translated from a manuscript in the British Library.

THE HAZARAS

The ethnic composition of Afghanistan is discussed in all the general accounts of the country. A book devoted to the Hazaras in particular is S. A. Mousavi, *The Hazaras of Afghanistan* (Richmond, 1998). The genetic research on the Hazaras is described in T. Zerjal et al., 'The genetic legacy of the Mongols', *American Journal of Human Genetics* 72 (2003), 717–21; and an excellent introduction to evolutionary genetics is L. L. Cavalli-Sforza, *Genes, Peoples and Languages* (London, 2000). A sensible interpretation of the historical evidence pertaining to the Hazaras is E. E. Bacon, 'The inquiry into the history of the Hazara Mongols of Afghanistan', *Southwestern Journal of Anthropology* 7 (1951), 230–47; and Hazaragi, the Hazara dialect of Persian, is analysed in G. K. Dulling, *The Hazaragi Dialect of Afghan Persian* (London, 1973). Wilfred Thesiger's investigation of Hazara culture is 'The Hazaras of central Afghanistan', *Geographical Journal* 121 (1955), 312–19. There is a succinct introduction to Shi'i Islam in Chapter 4 of M. Axworthy, *Iran: Empire of the Mind* (London, 2008); for more detail, see M. Momen, *An Introduction to Shi'i Islam* (New Haven and London, 1985). Hazara folklore concerning the Buddhas and Hazrat-i Ali is recorded in R. Hackin and A. A. Kohzad, *Légendes et coutumes afghans* (Paris, 1953).

Sturt's image of Shahr-i Zohak comes from R. H. Sale, *The Defence of Jellalabad* (1847). The Asiatick Society is described in J. M. Steadman, 'The Asiatick Society of Bengal', *Eighteenth-Century Studies* 10 (1977), 464–83 and M. J. Franklin, *Orientalist Jones* (Oxford, 2011). For the long and rich history of attempts to locate the Garden of Eden, see A. Scafi, *Mapping Paradise: A History of Heaven on Earth* (London, 2006). The first reference to the Buddhas of Bamiyan in the West was in Thomas Hyde's *Historia religionis veterum Persarum eorumque magorum* ('History of the Religion of the Ancient Persians and their Priests') of 1700, 132–3. Goethe's dismissal of the religious practices exemplified by Bamiyan is at *West-oestlicher Divan* (1819), 269. Highly readable general accounts of the rivalry between the Russian and British Empires are P. Hopkirk, *The Great Game* (London, 1990) and K. E. Meyer and S. B. Brysac, *Tournament of Shadows* (Washington, DC, 1999). An older but still interesting investigation of Western exploration of the area is T. H. Holdich, *The Gates of India* (London, 1910). The seminal historical treatment of British expansion towards the north-west of India is M. Yapp, *Strategies of British India* (Oxford, 1980).

The memoirs of the many European visitors to Bamiyan in the nineteenth century are these days in most cases easily accessible online, courtesy of Google Books, Internet Archive and other sites featuring scans of books out of copyright. Those cited here include: Mountstuart Elphinstone, *An Account of the Kingdom of Caubul* (1815); Rollo Burslem, *A Peep into Toorkisthan* (1846); Vincent Eyre, *The Military Operations at Cabul*, 3rd edn (1843); Lady Sale, *A Journal of the Disasters in Affghanistan, 1841–2* (1843); Revd Joseph Wolff, *Researches and Missionary Labours among the Jews, Mohammedans and Other Sects* (1837), *Narrative of a Mission to Bokhara* (1845), *Travels and Adventures of the Rev. Joseph Wolff* (1861); Alexander Burnes, *Travels into Bokhara* (1834), with General Court's letter of advice at vol. I, 33–8; G. T. Vigne, *A Personal Narrative of a Visit to Ghuzni, Kabul and Afghanistan* (1840); H. H. Wilson, *Travels in the Himalayan Provinces of Hindustan and the Panjab; in Ladakh and Kashmir; in Peshawar, Kabul, Kunduz, and Bokhara; by Mr. William Moorcroft and Mr. George Trebeck, from 1819–1825* (1841); Charles Masson, *Narrative of Various Journeys in Balochistan, Afghanistan and the Panjab*, vol. II (1842); Mohan Lal, *Travels in the Panjab, Afghanistan, Turkistan, to Balk, Bokhara, and Herat; and a visit to Great Britain and Germany* (1846); Josiah Harlan, *A Memoir of India and Avghanistaun* (1842); F. E. Ross (ed.), *Central Asia: Personal Narrative of General Josiah Harlan, 1823–1841* (London, 1939); J. L. Lee, *The Journals of Edward Stirling in Persia and Afghanistan, 1828–29* (Naples, 1991); J. A. Gray, *At the Court of the Amir* (1895).

The sources on individual actors, or on the wider scene, are usefully integrated in modern biographies and modern accounts of the so-called Great Game. A good life of Charles Masson is G. Whitteridge, *Charles Masson of Afghanistan* (Warminster, 1986), to which an addendum is G. L. Possehl, 'An archeological adventurer in Afghanistan: Charles Masson', *South Asian Studies* 6 (1990), 111–24. B. Macintyre, *Josiah the Great* (London, 2004), is an acute and vivid account of a man central to Afghan events in the run-up to the First Anglo-Afghan War. F. Maclean, *A Person from England* (London, 1958) has an excellent chapter on Joseph Wolff. Lady Sale's narrative is edited by P. A. Macrory (Oxford, 2002), who provides anecdotes of her celebrity; also useful is G. Pottinger and P. A. Macrory, *The Ten-rupee Jezail: Figures in the First Afghan War, 1838–42* (Norwich, 1993): Lady Sale's appearance in *Punch* is at 121–2 (to which add 'Punch's Lounge at the Exhibition of the Royal Academy', *Punch* (1845), 236–7). L. Colley, *Captives* (London, 2002), 347–66 places the experience of the British hostages in Afghanistan in the context of the long, inglorious history of British subjects in captivity.

Much of the discussion of Bamiyan was carried out in the pages of *Asiatick Researches* and its continuation, *Journal of the Asiatic Society of Bengal*, and indeed browsing any randomly chosen instalment of *JASB* in the 1830s is a good way to catch the ethos of the time. *Asiatick Researches* I (1789) contained William Jones's Third Anniversary Discourse (415–31); Francis Wilford's 'On Mount Caucasus' is in *Asiatick Researches* VI (1799), 455–539, and Reuben Burrow's intriguing theory about Stonehenge is in *Asiatick Researches* II (1791), 488. In the *Journal of the Asiatic Society of Bengal* are to be found a number of contributions by Charles Masson, notably 'Notes on the antiquities of Bamian', *JASB* 5 (1836), 707–20. The narrative based on Dr Gerard's letters describing his visit to Bamiyan is published at *JASB* 2 (1833), 1–22; and General Court's thoughts on Alexander's itinerary are at *JASB* 5 (1836), 387–95, and *Journal Asiatique* 4 (1837), 359–96. Mir Izzet Ullah's visit to Bamiyan during his reconnaissance of Moorcroft's route is described in the *Quarterly Oriental Magazine* 4.8 (1825), 296, and omitted at the *Journal of the Royal Asiatic Society of Great Britain and Ireland* 7 (1843), 342. Carl Ritter's discussion of Bamiyan is in *Die Stupa's (Topes) oder die architectonischen Denkmale an der Indo-Baktrischen Königsstraße* (1838), 19–69, and there is commentary in M. Mode, 'Ein vergessener Anfang: Carl Ritter und die "Kolosse von Bamiyan". Zum 220. Geburtstag des großen deutschen Geographen', www.orientarch.uni-halle. de/ca/bam/bamiyanx.htm.

C. M. Dorn'eich, *Minar-i-Chakari* (Kabul, 1999) is a study of the monument also known as the Minar-i Sikandar or Alexander's Pillar. R. Stoneman, *Alexander the Great: A Life in Legend* (New Haven and London, 2008) describes the mythological afterlife of Alexander, including in Afghanistan. Marco Polo's account of his travels is translated by R. E. Latham (London, 1958). Kipling's short story 'The Man Who Would Be King' was first published in *The Phantom Rickshaw and Other Eerie Tales* (1888) and later in *Wee Willie Winkie and Other Stories* (1895 and subsequent editions). A compelling treatment of Alexander's campaigns in Afghanistan, which seeks to draw out their contemporary resonances, is F. L. Holt, *Into the Land of Bones* (Berkeley, 2005).

THE TWENTIETH CENTURY

The recent history of Afghanistan, from the time of Abdur Rahman, is well presented by A. Rasanayagam, *Afghanistan: A Modern History* (New York and London, 2003); and that is the emphasis of an earlier classic, W. K. Fraser-Tytler, *Afghanistan: A Study of Political Developments in Central and Southern Asia*, 3rd edn (Oxford, 1967), which carried the story up to 1964. The activities of DAFA are described and richly illustrated in S. Gorshenina and C. Rapin, *De Kaboul à Samarcande* (Paris, 2001), and in the exhibition catalogue *Afghanistan: Les trésors retrouvés* (Paris, 2006). For the life and work of Aurel Stein, and an insight into the broader network of Buddhist sites he investigated in central Asia, see. J. Mirsky, *Sir Aurel Stein,*

Archaeological Explorer (Chicago, 1977) and S. Whitfield, *Aurel Stein on the Silk Road* (Chicago, 2004). Travel writers who visited Bamiyan include R. Byron, *The Road to Oxiana* (London, 1937); A. J. Toynbee, *Between Oxus and Jumna* (Oxford, 1961); F. Stark, *The Minaret of Djam* (London, 1970); P. Levi, *The Light Garden of the Angel King* (London, 1972); R. Stewart, *The Places in Between* (London, 2004). Bruce Chatwin's 'A lament for Afghanistan' is reprinted in *What Am I Doing Here?* (London, 1989), 286–93. Contrasting views on the ethics of the trade in antiquities are presented in O. Bopearachchi and F. Flandrin, *Le portrait d'Alexandre le Grand* (Monaco, 2005), a pacy description of the search for the coins and artefacts unearthed at Mir Zakah in 1992; and J. Braarvig and F. Liland, *Traces of Gandharan Buddhism: An Exhibition of Ancient Manuscripts in the Schøyen Collection* (Oslo, 2010). The Soviet war in Afghanistan is analysed from the Russian side by R. Braithwaite, *Afgantsy* (London, 2010); and the Afghan side by O. Roy, *Islam and Resistance in Afghanistan*, 2nd edn (Cambridge, 1990). A taste of Taliban enormities committed in Bamiyan during the civil war is provided by the report of 26 September 2001 to the UN General Assembly by Kamal Hossein, Special Rapporteur of the Commission on Human Rights, #A/56/409 (www.un.org/documents/ga/docs/56/a56409.pdf); UN report #A/53/539 (www.undemocracy.com/A-53-539.pdf) is a profoundly disturbing record of events in Mazar-i Sharif in 1998 by another Special Rapporteur, Choong-Hyun Paik. The work of mine clearers at Bamiyan and elsewhere in Afghanistan can begin to be appreciated from the excellent website of the Mine Action Coordination Centre of Afghanistan, www.macca.org.af/.

ILLUSTRATIONS

ACKNOWLEDGEMENTS

Regularly, in the course of writing this book, I have found myself in the position of asking dumb questions of highly intelligent people, and I am grateful for the friendly and generous responses my questions have almost invariably received. The following have all tried to help me get it right, and I can only offer my apologies to them if I haven't: Masashi Abi (National Research Institute for Cultural Properties, Japan), Mehrab Shah Afzali (MACCA), Mohammadjavad Ardalan, Arezou Azad, George Noel Clarke, Anna Collar and Ursula Sims-Williams (The Ancient India and Iran Trust), Richard Cooper, Paul Dennis, Nicolas Engel (DAFA), Marc Fautrez, Anna Garcia, Karl Gerth, Christa Gray, Peter Groves, Farrukh Husein, Rod Jackson, Sorna Khakzad, Jonathan Lee, Damon Lynch, Robert McChesney, Edmund Melzl, John Penney, Jaroslav Poncar, Tim Ramsey, Maggie Sasanow, Gianroberto Scarcia (for some exceptional help with bibliography), Eckhard Schiewek, J. Otto Seibold, Timor Sharan, Jake Simkin, Nicholas Sims-Williams, Flora Sutherland (MACCA), Peter Thonemann, and Chris Tyler-Smith. I am indebted also to the Jeffrey Fund at Brasenose College, Oxford for the extremely generous help they provided me in securing images.

That this project happened at all is the result of three surpassing acts of kindness: the decision of Peter Carson at Profile Books and the series editor Mary Beard to invite me to write it; my wife Andrea Swinton's willingness to let me travel in theoretically dangerous places; and above all Alan MacDonald's insistence that I should celebrate my fortieth birthday by seeing the Oxus at Ai Khanum. Getting to know what little I do now know about Afghanistan has been, and will always be, a highlight of my life, and the book that is the modest upshot of those trips to that remarkable country can only be for all of them.

INDEX

Figures in *italics* indicate
captions.

[221]

[224]

WONDERS OF THE WORLD

This is a small series of books that will focus on some of the world's most famous sites or monuments. Their names will be familiar to almost everyone: they have achieved iconic stature and are loaded with a fair amount of mythological baggage. These monuments have been the subject of many books over the centuries, but our aim, through the skill and stature of the writers, is to get something much more enlightening, stimulating, even controversial, than straightforward histories or guides. The series is under the general editorship of Mary Beard. Other titles in the series are:

Geremie R. Barmé: **The Forbidden City**
Mary Beard: **The Parthenon**
Gillian Darley: **Vesuvius**
Iain Fenlon: **Piazza San Marco**
Cathy Gere: **The Tomb of Agamemnon**
Simon Goldhill: **The Temple of Jerusalem**
Rosemary Hill: **Stonehenge**
Keith Hopkins & Mary Beard: **The Colosseum**
Robert Irwin: **The Alhambra**
Richard Jenkyns: **Westminster Abbey**
Keith Miller: **St Peter's**
John Ray: **The Rosetta Stone**
Giles Tillotson: **Taj Mahal**
David Watkin: **The Roman Forum**